The Trail From Vision To Mission

Joshua Rhoades

Published by Joshua Paul Rhoades, 2024.

While every precaution has been taken in the preparation of this book, the publisher assumes no responsibility for errors or omissions, or for damages resulting from the use of the information contained herein.

THE TRAIL FROM VISION TO MISSION

First edition. November 2, 2024.

Copyright © 2024 Joshua Rhoades.

ISBN: 979-8227054845

Written by Joshua Rhoades.

Also by Joshua Rhoades

Courage Under Fire: David's Stand On The Battlefield
Jonah's Journey: Voices Of Redemption And Lessons In Obedience
The Furnace Of Faith: 12 Principles From The Heat Of Faith
Whispers of Hope: Inspiring Stories of Men's Prayers In Scripture
Frontier Legends: The Oregon Dream
Elijah: A Beacon Of Boldness
HOOK, LINE & SAVIOUR - Faith Reflections from Fishing
Driven By Faith: Motor Racing Inspired Christian Life
30 Day Devotional - Bold and Strong- Coffee Devotions for a Courageous Christian Walk
Authentic Christianity: The Heart of Old Time Religion
Consider The Ant - God's Tiny Preachers
Flee Fornication: The Plea For Purity
Renewed Hope- How to Find Encouragement in God
Sounding The Call - The Voice of Conviction
The Altar - Where Heaven Meets Earth
The Bible's Battlefields- Timeless Lessons from Ancient Wars
The Sacred Art of Silence - How Silence Speaks in Scripture
Under Fire- The Sanctity of the Traditional Biblical Home
Who Is on the Lord's Side? A Call to Righteousness
What Is Truth? - From Skepticism to Submission
First and Goal- Faith and Football Fundamentals
From Dugout to Devotion- Spiritual Lessons from Baseball
Par for the Course- Faith and Fairways
The Believer's Pace- Tools for Running Life's Marathon
The Immutable Fortress- Security in God's Unchanging Nature
Biblical Bravery
Deer Stands and Devotions: A Hunter's Walk with God

Jesus Knows- Our Hearts, Our Responsibility
Restoration - Setting The Bone
Spiritual 911- God's Word for Life's Emergency's
The Freedom of Forgiveness
The Jezebel Effect - Ancient Manipulations Modern Lessons
The Shout That Stopped The Saviour
The Time Machine Chronicles: Old Testament Characters
Anchored In Truth Exploring The Depths of Psalm 119
Biblical Counsel on Anger
Proverbs' Portraits The Men God Mentions
Stumbling in the Dark - The Dangers of Alcohol
Guarding the Wicket Protecting Your Faith and Game
The Champion's Faith - Wrestling and Achieving Spiritual Victory
Scriptural Commands for Modern Times Living God's Word Today Volume 1
Scriptural Commands for Modern Times Living God's Word Today Volume 2
Scriptural Commands for Modern Times Living God's Word TodayVolume3
The Greatest Gift
A Christmas Journey of Faith
Daughter Of The King: Embracing Your Identity In Christ
Determination and Dedication Building Strong Faith As A Young Man
Walking Through Walls God's Power to Part the Storms of Life
David's Song Of Deliverance Praising God Through Every Storm
From Weakness to Warrior: Gideon's Transformation
Why Did Jesus Weep?
Living For God The Call To Be A Living Sacrifice
My Mind Is In A Fog What Do I Do?
Turning The Page Written By Grace
The Calling and Greatness of John the Baptist
For Such a Time Esther's Courageous Stand
From Brokenness To Beauty Written By The Pen of Grace
The Ultimate Guide to Massive Action- From Plans to Reality
A Heart Of Conviction
Serving In The Shadows
Repentance Revealed The Road Back To God
The Chief Sinner Meets The Chief Saviour Reflections On I Timothy 1:15

Answer The Call - 31 Days of Biblical Action
The Birthmark of the Believer
Reflections on Calvary's Cross
The Kingdom Builder Paul's Bold Proclamation of Christ
The Animal Of Pride
The Reach That Restores Christ Love For The Broken
Paul- The Many Roles of a Servant of Christ
Unshakeable Faith- 31 Days of Peace in God's Word
O Come, Let Us Adore Him- A Christmas Devotional
The Shepherd's Voice
The Trail From Vision To Mission

Dedication

To you, the reader of The Trail From Vision to Mission,

This book is dedicated to your courage, your compassion, and your faith. You hold in your hands not just a collection of words, but a guide that honors the sacred journey you've chosen to embark on. It's a journey that begins with seeing the world not just through your own eyes, but through the eyes of Christ, letting what you see affect your heart and stir you to action. This is no small decision. It's a calling that takes boldness and an openness to be moved, molded, and led by something greater than yourself.

To the one whose heart aches for something deeper, for a life that has meaning beyond the ordinary—this book is for you. It's for the person who looks at the world with a longing to make a difference, who sees need and wants to bring healing, who senses brokenness and desires to bring wholeness, and who, when faced with darkness, yearns to bring light. Your heart has been touched by the vision of a life lived for God, and that is something beautiful and rare. You are the reason this book was written.

May you find encouragement in these pages, and may you be reminded that this journey is not one you must travel alone. God is with you every step of the way, guiding you, equipping you, and giving you strength. This book is here to walk alongside you, to remind you that even when the path feels difficult, you are called and capable. It's okay to feel uncertain at times, to wonder if you're making a difference, or to question your abilities. But let this dedication be a gentle whisper to your soul: You are exactly where you are meant to be, and every step you take in faith is seen, cherished, and used by God for a purpose beyond what you can imagine.

You are here for a reason, and this journey—your journey—is of incredible worth. Each chapter in this book is crafted with you in mind, to help you discover new depths of your calling and to equip you for the mission God has laid on your heart. May you find strength when you feel weary, clarity when you face confusion, and joy in the small and sacred moments along the way.

This book is dedicated to the part of you that has heard God's call and responded with a resounding "yes." To the heart that is willing to be affected by what it sees, to the spirit ready to be shaped by God's hand, and to the soul longing to be poured out for the sake of others, this dedication is yours.

May "The Trail From Vision to Mission" be a source of hope, courage, and inspiration to you as you walk this path. Embrace this journey, knowing that every step, every act of love, and every moment of faith matters in ways that are eternal.

With every blessing, and with deep gratitude for the journey you're on, this book is lovingly dedicated to you.

Introduction
Chapter 1 – Transformation
Chapter 2 – Tenderness
Chapter 3 – Tenacity
Chapter 4 - Trust in God's Guidance
Chapter 5 – Testimony
Chapter 6 – Truthfulness
Chapter 7 – Teaching
Chapter 8 - Triumph Over Fear
Chapter 9 – Timeliness
Chapter 10 - Tuning In to God's Voice
Chapter 11 - Thirst for Righteousness
Chapter 12 – Tenderheartedness
Chapter 13 - Taking Initiative
Chapter 14 – Trustworthiness
Chapter 15 - Total Surrender
Chapter 16 - Triumphant Spirit
Chapter 17 - Tempered with Grace
Chapter 18 - Thriving in Faith
Chapter 19 - Tactical Wisdom
Chapter 20 - Taking Heart
Chapter 21 - Truth as Foundation
Chapter 22 - Turning from Distractions
Chapter 23 - Teaching by Example
Chapter 24 - Total Dependence on God
Chapter 25 - Treasuring the Call
Conclusion

Introduction

Welcome to "The Trail from Vision to Mission," a journey rooted in the powerful words of Lamentations 3:51: "Mine eye affecteth mine heart." In these words, we find a profound truth: what we see has the power to move us deeply, to stir our hearts, and to inspire us to action. When God opens our eyes to the needs around us and the purposes He has placed within us, it transforms not only our perspective but also our priorities. As our eyes take in the world through His lens, our hearts are touched with compassion, our spirits awakened, and we feel an undeniable calling to step forward and serve.

This book offers a pathway for those who feel the stirring of a greater purpose, who recognize that their Christian life is meant to be more than passive faith. Through 25 chapters, "The Trail from Vision to Mission" explores what it means to turn a heartfelt vision into intentional, impactful mission. Each chapter is designed to help you respond to God's calling, equipping you to put faith into action and to live a life that reflects His love. Starting with the clarity that comes from truly seeing—both ourselves and others as God does—this journey unfolds as a practical guide to deepen your spiritual walk and engage in meaningful service.

In these pages, you'll find more than just encouragement; you'll find specific steps to help you develop the qualities and mindset needed to carry out God's vision for your life. You'll learn the importance of cultivating compassion, humility, and perseverance as you walk this path. Each chapter addresses a unique aspect of living out God's calling, from understanding the power of faith-driven vision to taking actionable steps toward your mission. Along the way, you'll discover that every step of obedience, every act of service, and every moment spent in God's presence strengthens you, preparing you to be a more effective servant in His Kingdom.

This book isn't just for those who feel called to full-time ministry or missions. "The Trail from Vision to Mission" speaks to every believer who desires to make a difference in the world, no matter their role, background, or location. You don't have to be in a distant land or stand behind a pulpit to make an impact; God's mission field is wherever He has placed you—your family, workplace, community, and beyond. In each of these areas, you have the opportunity to bring the light of Christ, to influence lives, and to fulfill a mission that is unique to you.

As you embark on this journey, let your heart remain open to the ways God may guide you, refine you, and stretch you. May these chapters inspire you to let your vision shape your heart and lead you to action. Together, we'll explore the steps from seeing to doing, from knowing to responding, and from vision to mission. So take a deep breath, prepare your heart, and get ready to experience the life God has designed for you—a life filled with purpose, guided by vision, and set on a mission that reflects His love and transforms lives.

Chapter 1 – Transformation

The journey on the "Trail From Vision to Mission" begins with transformation, where seeing the needs of others changes our hearts and calls us to action, as the Bible says in Romans 12:2, "And be not conformed to this world: but be ye transformed by the renewing of your mind, that ye may prove what is that good, and acceptable, and perfect, will of God." When we open our eyes to see the struggles and burdens people carry, something shifts within us. We can no longer remain distant; instead, our hearts grow tender, our thoughts deepen, and we feel moved to help. This is more than just feeling sorry for others—it's a compassionate stirring that challenges us to do something about it. The Bible tells us that Jesus was often moved with compassion when He saw the crowds, as in Matthew 9:36, where He looked on them with care because they were like sheep without a shepherd. Like Jesus, when we are moved by compassion, our focus changes. We start to care about people beyond their outward appearance, looking deeper into their hearts and understanding their needs. Compassion transforms our perspective, just as Jesus looked upon Zacchaeus, a man despised by others, with eyes of love and acceptance. Transformation begins when we stop looking through the lens of judgment and start seeing through the lens of love. This change in perspective brings us closer to fulfilling the mission God has called us to, as we can now see clearly what He wants us to do.

Compassion moves us to take steps that we may not have thought possible before. When we see someone in pain or struggling, we begin to want to help them, whether it's by giving, praying, or spending time with them. James 2:15-16 reminds us, "If a brother or sister be naked, and destitute of daily food, and one of you say unto them, Depart in peace, be ye warmed and filled; notwithstanding ye give them not those things which are needful to the body; what doth it profit?" This means that compassion is not just about feeling but about action. If our vision of others' needs stirs our hearts, it should lead us to act in ways that make a difference. By taking these steps, we fulfill our mission as Christians, demonstrating God's love in practical ways. We find ourselves willing to do more, to go further, and to give what we have to help others because our hearts are no longer hard. God calls us to live out our faith through acts of kindness and generosity, which is why the trail from vision to mission is filled with opportunities to show His love to others.

As we continue on this trail, we start to realize that transformation doesn't just happen outwardly but also inwardly. As we act on behalf of others, our own hearts change as well. The Bible speaks about the need to "put on a heart of compassion, kindness, humility, meekness, and patience" in Colossians 3:12, which shows us that our character becomes more like Christ when we help others. Our mission becomes more than just an obligation; it becomes a joy, a calling, and a purpose. In seeing the needs of others, we become less focused on ourselves and more aware of the world around us. Instead of seeking our own comfort or desires, we seek ways to comfort and serve others, showing them the love that God has given us. Transformation is a journey, and every time we step forward to help, we are drawn closer to God's heart. Jesus Himself said that when we care for "the least of these" (Matthew 25:40), we are serving Him directly. So, every kind word, every selfless action, and every gift of time or resources we give in Jesus' name brings us further along the trail from vision to mission.

As we go deeper into this mission, our faith is strengthened. Each step of obedience teaches us to trust God more, as we see Him working through us to reach others. Proverbs 3:5-6 encourages us to "trust in the Lord with all thine heart; and lean not unto thine own understanding. In all thy ways acknowledge him, and he shall direct thy paths." We learn that when we place our trust in God, He will lead us to where we need to go, equipping us for the work He has prepared for us. We don't always know the impact we're making, but God does, and He blesses our efforts, no matter how small they may seem. By allowing our hearts to be transformed and following where God leads, we become vessels of His love, helping to change lives and bring hope. This is the true mission: to let our vision of others' needs guide us to take action, just as Jesus did. Transformation isn't always easy, and there will be times when we might feel inadequate or afraid. But God reminds us, as He did Joshua, to "be strong and of a good courage" (Joshua 1:9), because He is with us every step of the way.

On this trail from vision to mission, we also discover the importance of humility. We realize that we are only instruments in God's hands, and without His guidance, our efforts would be in vain. Jesus demonstrated humility when He washed His disciples' feet, showing them that true greatness comes from serving others (John 13:14-15). As we follow His example, we come to understand that our mission is not about us or about gaining recognition; it's about bringing glory to God and showing others His love. Transformation through compassion teaches us that even the smallest acts can have a big impact when done in love. Galatians 6:9 reminds us, "And let us not be weary in well doing: for in due season we shall reap, if we faint not." We are encouraged to keep going, even when the road seems long or the results are slow to appear. Every small act of kindness, every prayer, and every moment spent listening to someone in need is a step forward on this trail.

In the end, the trail from vision to mission is not just a path we walk for others, but a path that changes us too. Our hearts grow stronger, our faith becomes more steadfast, and our love becomes more genuine. We become reflections of God's compassion in a world that desperately needs hope. This journey teaches us the importance of seeing others through God's eyes, feeling their pain, and responding with a heart of love and service. By embracing this mission, we fulfill Jesus' command in Acts 1:8, where He said, "Ye shall be witnesses unto me." We become witnesses not just in words but in deeds, showing the world who Jesus is by the way we live. As we walk this trail, we find ourselves closer to God, transformed by His love and committed to making a difference, one person at a time. This is the beautiful purpose of the trail from vision to mission—to allow God's love to transform us so we can transform the world around us, bringing glory to Him in all we do.

Chapter 2 – Tenderness

The journey on the "Trail From Vision to Mission" begins with tenderness. When God opens our eyes to see the needs around us, He gives us a heart full of gentleness and kindness. This tenderness is not weakness, but a powerful compassion that moves us to help others in ways we may not have before. Ephesians 4:32 reminds us to "be ye kind one to another, tenderhearted, forgiving one another, even as God for Christ's sake hath forgiven you." This verse shows that true kindness comes from a tender heart that understands the pain, struggles, and burdens of others. When we feel tenderhearted, we are less likely to judge or criticize; instead, we feel empathy and understanding. We remember that we all have weaknesses and need God's grace. Tenderness opens our eyes to see beyond the surface, seeing people for who they truly are, with all their joys and sorrows. Jesus was often moved with compassion when He saw people suffering, and this compassion led Him to heal, teach, and feed them. His tenderness was an active love that reached out to people, touching their lives in real ways. In the same way, our vision of others' needs should lead us to take action, to show kindness, and to be patient.

When we are tenderhearted, we become more aware of the silent struggles people carry. Many people may look fine on the outside but are hurting on the inside, and a kind word or gentle touch can make a world of difference. Tenderness allows us to look past our own needs and focus on helping others, whether it's through words, actions, or just being there for someone in a time of need. The Bible tells us in Colossians 3:12, "Put on therefore, as the elect of God, holy and beloved, bowels of mercies, kindness, humbleness of mind, meekness, longsuffering." This verse reminds us that being tenderhearted is part of being God's chosen people; it's part of living a life that reflects His love. When we are tender, we become more like Christ, who was gentle and humble in heart. We stop seeing others as obstacles or problems and start seeing them as people God loves and cares for deeply. Tenderness helps us listen better, love deeper, and forgive more easily. It teaches us to be patient with those who are difficult, to encourage those who are struggling, and to help those who are hurting.

Tenderness doesn't just change the way we see others; it also changes us. As we grow in kindness and empathy, we become more sensitive to the Holy Spirit's guidance. We begin to feel God's love for people in a new way, a way that goes beyond words and actions. This kind of love motivates us to be God's hands and feet in the world, reaching out to those in need. The Bible tells us in James 2:15-16, "If a brother or sister be naked, and destitute of daily food, and one of you say unto them, Depart in peace, be ye warmed and filled; notwithstanding ye give them not those things which are needful to the body; what doth it profit?" This scripture reminds us that tenderness is more than just feeling sympathy; it's about taking real steps to help others. If we see someone who is cold or hungry, it's not enough to just wish them well; we are called to do what we can to meet their needs. True tenderness moves us to act, to give, and to share. It makes us generous and selfless, putting the needs of others before our own comfort. We realize that our time, resources, and talents are gifts from God, meant to be used to bless others.

The trail from vision to mission is marked by moments when our hearts are softened, when we feel the gentle nudge of God's love urging us to reach out. Every act of kindness, every word of encouragement, and every gift of love we give is a step along this trail. We are reminded of 1 John 3:18, "My little children, let us not love in word, neither in tongue; but in deed and in truth." This means that our love should be real, shown in the things we do, not just in what we say. When our vision is filled with tenderness, we don't hold back from helping others; we go the extra mile to show them they are valued and loved. Tenderness teaches us to serve without expecting anything in return, to give freely as Jesus gave to us. We remember that Jesus said, "It is more blessed to give than to receive" (Acts 20:35). This spirit of giving brings us joy and fulfills our purpose as followers of Christ. We find that in helping others, we are also blessed, growing closer to God and feeling His presence more deeply in our lives.

As we walk the trail from vision to mission, we find that tenderness leads to peace. When we live with a heart full of kindness and compassion, we experience a deep sense of satisfaction and contentment. We are not weighed down by anger or resentment because tenderness has taught us to forgive. We let go of grudges and choose to love, even when it's hard. Philippians 4:7 tells us about "the peace of God, which passeth all understanding," which comes when we live according to God's love. This peace fills our hearts when we are tenderhearted, when we treat others with kindness, and when we choose to look at people through the eyes of grace. Our mission becomes clearer, not because we have all the answers, but because we know that God's love will guide us. Tenderness makes our hearts soft and receptive, helping us hear God's voice more clearly and feel His presence more closely.

At the end of the day, the trail from vision to mission is a journey of love. It's a path that leads us to become more like Christ, showing His kindness and compassion in everything we do. Every step we take, every act of kindness we give, and every moment we spend caring for others brings us closer to fulfilling the mission God has for us. We begin to see that our lives are not about gaining wealth, fame, or success, but about loving others and making a difference in their lives. We find joy in lifting others up, in being a light in dark places, and in spreading God's love wherever we go. This is the true purpose of our lives as Christians: to be a reflection of Christ's love, to be tenderhearted and kind, and to make the world a better place one person at a time.

The Bible tells us in Matthew 5:7, "Blessed are the merciful: for they shall obtain mercy." This beatitude reminds us that as we show mercy and tenderness to others, we also receive God's mercy in our own lives. Tenderness is a gift that grows the more we give it, and each act of kindness strengthens our hearts and brings us closer to God. As we walk this trail, we learn that tenderness is not just something we feel but something we do. It's a way of life, a choice to be kind, gentle, and loving, even when it's difficult. It's about seeing the world through God's eyes, feeling His compassion, and sharing it with others. The trail from vision to mission is not always easy, but it's a journey worth taking. It's a path that leads to true happiness, peace, and fulfillment, knowing that we are doing God's work and making a difference in the lives of those around us.

In the end, tenderness is the heart of our mission. It's the foundation of all that we do, the reason we reach out, and the purpose behind every act of kindness. When our hearts are tender, we are open to God's leading, willing to be used by Him, and ready to serve. We become like Jesus, who was "moved with compassion" (Matthew 9:36) and reached out to those in need. This is the call for every believer: to walk the trail from vision to mission, guided by tenderness, and to make a lasting impact in the lives of others. This is the way of love, the way of Christ, and the way we are called to live.

Chapter 3 – Tenacity

The journey on the "Trail From Vision to Mission" calls us to have tenacity, a deep determination that helps us keep going, even when things get hard, so that we can share God's love with others. When we feel a vision in our hearts, something that truly moves us, we gain a sense of purpose that pushes us forward, and it's this tenacity that helps us keep walking along the path God has set for us. The Bible tells us in Galatians 6:9, "And let us not be weary in well doing: for in due season we shall reap, if we faint not." This means that even when the work seems difficult or when we feel tired, we should not give up, because God promises that our efforts are not in vain; there will be fruit, there will be a harvest, if we remain steadfast. Tenacity is important because, along this journey, we will face obstacles. We may feel discouraged, misunderstood, or even face opposition, but tenacity gives us the strength to keep going, knowing that what we are doing is meaningful. Jesus Himself showed tenacity when He walked the earth, never giving up on people, even when they doubted Him, rejected Him, or misunderstood Him. He kept sharing God's love, kept healing, kept teaching, and ultimately went to the cross for us. His example of never giving up, of holding onto His mission with unwavering determination, shows us that tenacity is an essential part of fulfilling our calling.

When our hearts are truly moved by God's love, we are filled with a determination that comes from Him, and this helps us overcome challenges. Tenacity doesn't mean we won't feel tired or discouraged at times, but it means we won't let those feelings stop us. Instead, we find strength in God to keep going, to keep sharing His love, and to keep making a difference. The Bible reminds us in 2 Timothy 1:7, "For God hath not given us the spirit of fear; but of power, and of love, and of a sound mind." This verse tells us that we do not have to be afraid or lose heart, because God has given us power and love.

With this tenacity, we find courage to speak up for what is right, to share our faith with others, and to keep doing good works, even when the world around us doesn't always support us. The world may sometimes seem indifferent or even hostile to the message of God's love, but tenacity helps us to stand firm, not swayed by the opinions of others, because we know that God's truth is unchanging. Jesus said in Matthew 5:16, "Let your light so shine before men, that they may see your good works, and glorify your Father which is in heaven." Tenacity allows our light to shine, helping us to be a beacon of hope in a world that often feels dark and uncertain. We continue to serve, to love, to reach out, knowing that our actions reflect God's love and point others toward Him.

Tenacity also reminds us that success isn't always immediate. Sometimes, we may not see the results of our efforts right away, and this can be discouraging. We might wonder if what we're doing even matters, or if anyone is paying attention. But tenacity teaches us to keep sowing seeds of kindness, of compassion, and of truth, because we trust that in God's timing, those seeds will grow. The Bible speaks about this in Ecclesiastes 3:1, "To every thing there is a season, and a time to every purpose under the heaven." This means that there is a purpose and a timing for everything, and we may not always understand it right now, but God does. Our tenacity is rooted in faith, believing that God is working through us, even when we can't see the results. It teaches us patience and endurance, two qualities that are important as we walk the trail from vision to mission. This is a journey, not a sprint, and tenacity is what helps us to walk steadily, trusting that God is guiding our steps and using our efforts for His glory.

When we are tenacious, we learn to rely on God's strength rather than our own. There will be days when we feel weak or when we feel like giving up, but tenacity calls us to turn to God, to pray, and to ask for His strength. Philippians 4:13 tells us, "I can do all things through Christ which strengtheneth me." This verse reminds us that we are not walking this path alone; Christ is with us, empowering us to keep going, to keep sharing, and to keep loving. Tenacity in our mission means that we don't let setbacks or failures define us. Instead, we learn from them and keep moving forward. Every step, every act of love, every prayer, and every moment spent helping others is part of a larger picture that God is creating. We may not see it all now, but tenacity keeps us faithful, knowing that God's plan is bigger than we can imagine. As we persevere, we grow in character and strength. Romans 5:3-4 says, "And not only so, but we glory in tribulations also: knowing that tribulation worketh patience; And patience, experience; and experience, hope." This shows that the challenges we face along the way build us up, making us stronger and giving us hope. Through every difficulty, God is shaping us, refining our faith, and helping us to become more like Christ.

On this trail from vision to mission, tenacity also helps us to inspire others. When people see us holding on to our faith, staying committed to our calling, and loving others with consistency, it encourages them to do the same. Tenacity isn't just about personal perseverance; it's about being a role model for others, showing them that with God, they too can overcome obstacles. As we hold fast to our mission, we become examples to those around us, especially to younger generations who may be looking for guidance. Our tenacity sends a message that following God is worth it, even when it's hard, and that His love is a treasure that we can share with others. Hebrews 10:23 encourages us, "Let us hold fast the profession of our faith without wavering; (for he is faithful that promised)." By staying committed, we demonstrate that God's promises are true, and we encourage others to hold fast to their faith as well. Every time we choose to keep going, every time we decide to show love instead of giving up, we are showing others what it means to truly follow Christ.

Tenacity also reminds us of the importance of small, daily acts of kindness. Sometimes, our mission doesn't involve big, dramatic actions but simple acts of love and kindness that, over time, make a huge difference. Jesus said in Matthew 10:42, "And whosoever shall give to drink unto one of these little ones a cup of cold water only in the name of a disciple, verily I say unto you, he shall in no wise lose his reward." This tells us that even the smallest gestures matter to God. Tenacity is about showing up every day, doing what we can with what we have, and trusting that God is using even our smallest actions to build His kingdom. It's about being faithful in the little things, knowing that they add up to something big in God's eyes. When we serve with tenacity, we are planting seeds of love and hope that will grow and flourish in ways we may never see.

Ultimately, the trail from vision to mission is a journey of faith, perseverance, and love. It's a path that requires us to be strong, to trust in God, and to keep moving forward, no matter what obstacles we face. Tenacity is what keeps us grounded, reminding us of why we started this journey in the first place and helping us to stay focused on our mission. We remember that Jesus Himself faced challenges, but He never gave up, because He was driven by love for us. Our tenacity is a reflection of His love, a reminder that we are called to keep going, to keep sharing, and to keep loving, no matter what. This is the essence of the trail from vision to mission: a path where we walk with courage, guided by faith, empowered by God's love, and strengthened by a tenacious spirit that refuses to give up. With every step, we grow closer to God, and we draw others closer to Him as well, making a lasting impact in the world around us.

Chapter 4 - Trust in God's Guidance

The journey on the "Trail From Vision to Mission" is built on trust in God's guidance, knowing that He will lead us each step of the way as we follow His calling. Proverbs 3:5-6 reminds us, "Trust in the Lord with all thine heart; and lean not unto thine own understanding. In all thy ways acknowledge him, and he shall direct thy paths." This means that even when we don't understand everything, when things seem uncertain or even difficult, God has a perfect plan, and we can trust Him to guide us. Trusting in God's guidance means that we don't have to figure it all out on our own; we can lean on His wisdom, knowing that He sees what we cannot. Our vision, the things we feel called to do, grows clearer as we put our trust in God, because He directs us and opens doors at the right time. Trusting in God means being willing to let go of our own fears and doubts, choosing to believe that God is faithful and will make a way. He may not show us the whole path at once, but as we take each step in faith, He reveals more of His plan. Just like how a lantern lights up the next few steps of a dark path, God's guidance shines enough light for us to keep moving forward, even if we can't see the whole journey.

Along this trail, there will be moments when we feel unsure or anxious, when we face obstacles or times when we wonder if we're on the right path. But trust in God's guidance reminds us that we are never alone. The Bible says in Isaiah 41:10, "Fear thou not; for I am with thee: be not dismayed; for I am thy God: I will strengthen thee; yea, I will help thee; yea, I will uphold thee with the right hand of my righteousness." This verse reassures us that God is with us, supporting us and helping us, even in the tough moments. Trusting in Him means we don't have to carry the weight of our mission alone; we can rely on His strength. There is comfort in knowing that God has a perfect plan, and even if things don't always go as we expect, He is still in control. When we trust in God's guidance, we find peace, because we know that His ways are higher than our ways, and His thoughts are higher than our thoughts (Isaiah 55:8-9). We begin to understand that God's timing is perfect, and that He is always working behind the scenes, arranging things in ways we might not understand but are always for our good and His glory.

Trusting God's guidance also means being open to His leading in unexpected ways. Sometimes, we may think we know what's best, but God, who sees the bigger picture, may lead us in a different direction. This is where humility comes in, acknowledging that we don't know everything and that we need God's wisdom. James 1:5 says, "If any of you lack wisdom, let him ask of God, that giveth to all men liberally, and upbraideth not; and it shall be given him." When we ask for God's guidance, He promises to give it freely. Trusting in God's guidance means we listen for His voice, sometimes in the quiet moments, through prayer, reading His Word, or through wise counsel from others who walk in faith. God can use many ways to guide us, and our part is to be open and willing to follow where He leads, even if it's not where we expected to go. As we trust Him, He gives us peace in our hearts, confirming His direction and giving us confidence to move forward.

On this journey from vision to mission, trust in God's guidance also builds patience in us. There are times when we may feel eager to move forward quickly, but God's timing is different from ours. Sometimes He asks us to wait, to be still, and to trust that He is preparing the way. Psalm 27:14 says, "Wait on the Lord: be of good courage, and he shall strengthen thine heart: wait, I say, on the Lord." Waiting can be hard, especially when we feel passionate about our mission, but trusting in God's guidance means believing that He knows the perfect timing. While we wait, God often uses this time to prepare our hearts, to teach us things we need to learn, and to strengthen our faith. Trusting God during these times helps us grow spiritually, making us stronger and more equipped for the work ahead. We learn that sometimes the journey itself, with all its waiting and growing, is just as important as the destination.

Trusting in God's guidance on this trail also reminds us to surrender our own plans and desires, allowing God to lead. Proverbs 16:9 says, "A man's heart deviseth his way: but the Lord directeth his steps." This means that while we may have plans, God is the one who ultimately directs our steps. Surrendering our plans to God doesn't mean we lose our dreams; instead, it means we let God shape them according to His perfect will. It's a process of letting go, of saying,

"Lord, not my will, but Thine be done." In doing this, we find that God's plans are often greater than what we could have imagined for ourselves. Trusting in His guidance helps us let go of control, releasing our worries, and choosing to believe that God's path is the best path, even when it's different from what we had envisioned.

This trust in God's guidance also brings a sense of purpose to our mission. We realize that we are part of something bigger than ourselves, a plan that God has been orchestrating since the beginning of time. Ephesians 2:10 tells us, "For we are his workmanship, created in Christ Jesus unto good works, which God hath before ordained that we should walk in them." This verse shows that God has a specific purpose for each of us, and as we trust in His guidance, we step into that purpose, becoming part of His work in the world. Our mission becomes not just something we do, but a calling from God, a way to live out the purpose He has placed in our hearts. Trusting in God's guidance makes our steps firm, giving us confidence that we are exactly where we need to be, doing the work God has prepared for us.

As we walk this trail from vision to mission, trusting in God's guidance brings us closer to Him. We learn to depend on Him daily, to seek His wisdom, and to listen for His voice. Trusting God is not a one-time decision; it's a daily choice to lean on Him, to ask for His direction, and to believe that He will lead us. Psalm 32:8 says, "I will instruct thee and teach thee in the way which thou shalt go: I will guide thee with mine eye." This promise assures us that God is watching over us, guiding us with His loving eye, leading us step by step. The more we trust Him, the stronger our faith becomes, and the more we see His hand at work in our lives. We start to recognize that God's guidance is not just about leading us to a destination, but about shaping us, teaching us, and drawing us closer to Him along the way.

Ultimately, the trail from vision to mission is a journey of trust, learning to rely on God's guidance every step of the way. It's about letting go of our own understanding, surrendering our plans, and choosing to believe that God knows best. As we walk in faith, trusting that God will lead us, we find peace, purpose, and a deep assurance that we are part of His plan. This journey teaches us that trust in God's guidance is the foundation of our mission, giving us the courage to step out, the patience to wait, and the confidence to follow wherever He leads. We learn that trusting in God's guidance is more than just a part of our journey; it's the heart of our relationship with Him, a daily act of faith that brings us closer to fulfilling the mission He has placed in our hearts. As we continue on this trail, may we remember that God is always with us, guiding us, and leading us to accomplish His purpose, for His glory and our good.

Chapter 5 – Testimony

The journey on the "Trail From Vision to Mission" is enriched by the power of testimony, where affected hearts inspire us to share what God has done in our lives, reaching out to those in need with compassion and hope. A testimony is simply the story of how God has worked in our lives, and sharing it is one of the most powerful ways to make an impact. Psalm 66:16 says, "Come and hear, all ye that fear God, and I will declare what he hath done for my soul." When we share our testimonies, we open a door for others to see God's love, faithfulness, and power at work, not just in history or scripture, but in our own lives. Testimony turns our faith into something real and relatable, connecting us with others in a personal way. It allows us to show people that God cares, that He is active in our lives, and that He is ready to work in theirs too. Each of us has a unique story—a story of how God reached us, saved us, guided us, healed us, or changed us. When we allow our hearts to be affected by the needs of those around us, we feel moved to share these stories, knowing they could bring hope to someone who is struggling.

The power of testimony is that it is honest and personal; it does not require a deep knowledge of theology or special training. Instead, it's about sharing from the heart, showing others what God has done and continues to do in our lives. When we tell others how God has helped us overcome challenges, how He has given us peace, or how He has provided for us in times of need, we are witnessing to His goodness. Our testimonies become a bridge, connecting our hearts with those who are hurting, questioning, or feeling lost. It's amazing how our personal experiences, even those we might see as small or unimportant, can make a huge difference to someone else. God can use the ordinary moments in our lives—the struggles, the victories, and everything in between—to reach people in extraordinary ways. Sometimes, a simple story of God's faithfulness can inspire others to trust Him, even in the midst of their own struggles. By sharing what God has done for us, we let people know that they are not alone, that others have faced similar battles, and that there is hope.

A testimony is not only a story of our past but a declaration of God's presence in our lives today. It's a reminder that the God who was with us yesterday is the same God who will be with us tomorrow. This assurance can bring incredible comfort to others, especially those who may be going through difficult times. In Revelation 12:11, it says, "And they overcame him by the blood of the Lamb, and by the word of their testimony." This shows that our testimonies have the power to defeat the darkness, to bring light into the lives of those who need it most. Sharing our stories of God's work is a way to spread hope, to let others know that God is still in control, still loving, and still working in our lives. It's a way to shine His light in a world that often feels dark and uncertain. Our testimonies remind others that no matter what they are going through, God is able to bring them through it, just as He has done for us.

Testimonies also encourage us, strengthening our own faith as we recall all that God has done. When we share our story, we are reminded of God's faithfulness, His grace, and His mercy. This strengthens our trust in Him, deepening our relationship with Him. Sometimes, sharing our testimony is not just for others—it's for us, too. It helps us remember how far we've come, how much God has done, and how faithful He has been through every season of our lives. As we speak about God's goodness, our gratitude grows, and our faith becomes more rooted in Him. It's as if we are re-living those moments of grace and love all over again, and this fuels our faith for the future. By sharing, we are also declaring our confidence in God, that He who began a good work in us will carry it on to completion (Philippians 1:6). Each time we give testimony, we are planting seeds of faith in others and reaffirming our own commitment to God.

Our testimonies can be a source of comfort and encouragement for those who are struggling, those who may feel like giving up. Many people feel like they are alone in their pain, but when we share our stories, they see that they are not alone. We have all been through challenges, faced fears, and struggled with doubts, but our testimonies show that God was with us every step of the way. By opening up about our own struggles and victories, we give others the courage to keep going, to hold on to hope, and to believe that things can get better. Proverbs 27:17 says, "Iron sharpeneth iron; so a man sharpeneth the countenance of his friend." This verse reminds us that by sharing our stories, we help each other grow stronger. We build each other up, encouraging one another to keep trusting in God. Testimonies bring us closer together, reminding us that we are all part of God's family, supporting each other as we walk this journey of faith.

In sharing our testimonies, we become witnesses to God's love. Jesus called us to be His witnesses in Acts 1:8, saying, "But ye shall receive power, after that the Holy Ghost is come upon you: and ye shall be witnesses unto me." A witness is someone who tells what they have seen and experienced, and that's exactly what a testimony is. It's telling others what we have experienced with God, showing them that He is real and that His love is life-changing. Our testimonies are like living proof of God's love, mercy, and power. We are not just talking about a distant God but a God who is active and involved in our daily lives. By sharing our stories, we let others see God's work in us, and this can open their hearts to experience Him as well. It's a way to glorify God, to lift His name, and to show the world the difference He makes in our lives. Every time we share what God has done, we are giving Him honor and pointing others to His grace.

The beauty of testimony is that it's ongoing. God's work in our lives doesn't stop; He is constantly shaping, guiding, and teaching us. Each new experience, each answered prayer, and each act of grace adds to our story. Our testimonies grow and deepen as we continue to walk with God, giving us even more to share with others. We never run out of reasons to praise Him, because His blessings are new every morning (Lamentations 3:22-23). This means that our mission to share our testimonies is never finished; there will always be someone who needs to hear, someone who needs encouragement, and someone who needs to know that God loves them. We are called to keep sharing, to keep testifying, to keep reaching out, because there are always hearts in need of hope.

Ultimately, the trail from vision to mission, powered by testimony, is a path of love. It's about loving others enough to open our hearts, to be vulnerable, and to share our experiences in a way that points them to God. It's about reaching out to those in need, whether they are hurting, lost, or searching, and offering them the hope we have found in Christ. It's about showing them that God cares, that He is near, and that He can change their lives just as He has changed ours. Every testimony is a gift, a way to spread light, hope, and love. It's a way to invite others to experience God for themselves, to know His love, and to walk with Him. As we continue on this trail, may we remember the power of our stories, the impact of our testimonies, and the mission to reach out, one heart at a time, sharing God's love with the world.

Chapter 6 – Truthfulness

The journey on the "Trail From Vision to Mission" requires truthfulness, a quality that goes beyond just telling the truth. It means being honest, genuine, and transparent in all we do, especially as we share God's love with others. Ephesians 4:15 says, "But speaking the truth in love, may grow up into him in all things, which is the head, even Christ." This verse teaches us that truthfulness, when combined with love, helps us grow to be more like Jesus. Truthfulness shows that we care enough about others to be open and sincere with them. It means that we don't just tell people what they want to hear, but what they need to hear, always in a spirit of kindness and respect. When we are truthful, we reflect God's heart, for He is the source of all truth. The Bible tells us in John 14:6 that Jesus said, "I am the way, the truth, and the life," and by following His example, we bring light to the world, a light that shines through honesty and integrity.

Truthfulness helps us build trust in our relationships with others, making them feel safe and valued. When people see that we are genuine, that we mean what we say, and that we care about them, they are more likely to open up and share their own struggles and questions. This honesty creates a space where people feel free to be themselves, to ask questions, and to seek God's truth. In a world where it can sometimes be hard to know what is real, being truthful stands out as a powerful witness to God's unchanging love. We're called to show people that God's truth is reliable and that His promises are sure. When we live truthfully, we show others that God's word is not just something we read, but something we live by every day. Proverbs 12:22 says, "Lying lips are abomination to the Lord: but they that deal truly are his delight." This verse shows us that truthfulness brings joy to God, and when we strive to be truthful, we please Him.

Walking in truthfulness also means being honest with ourselves and with God. Sometimes, we might be tempted to hide our mistakes, to pretend we have it all together, or to put on a mask for others. But true honesty begins with admitting our weaknesses, bringing our struggles to God, and asking for His help. 1 John 1:9 reminds us, "If we confess our sins, he is faithful and just to forgive us our sins, and to cleanse us from all unrighteousness." This means that when we are truthful with God, He forgives us and helps us to grow. Being honest with ourselves and with God helps us to become stronger, more compassionate, and more understanding of others' struggles. It reminds us that we are all in need of God's grace, and this humility allows us to connect with others on a deeper level. When people see that we are real about our own struggles, they feel encouraged to be real about theirs, knowing they won't be judged but accepted and loved.

Truthfulness is also about speaking God's truth to others, even when it's difficult. Sometimes, sharing the truth means saying things that may not be easy to hear, but if done in love, it can bring healing and growth. Ephesians 4:29 encourages us, "Let no corrupt communication proceed out of your mouth, but that which is good to the use of edifying, that it may minister grace unto the hearers." This means that our words should build others up, bringing grace and encouragement, not tearing them down. When we speak the truth in love, we are not trying to hurt or criticize, but to help others grow closer to God. Being truthful also means we don't just flatter or agree with people to please them; we tell the truth because we care about their well-being. Real love doesn't shy away from the truth; instead, it finds a gentle, respectful way to say it, hoping that it will lead to a positive change.

Truthfulness in our mission also means standing up for what is right, even when it's hard. In a world where truth can often be twisted, where people may go along with things they know are wrong just to fit in, being truthful means having the courage to stand up for God's ways. It means being a light in the darkness, showing others that God's truth is unchanging, and that His ways are good. Jesus said in Matthew 5:16, "Let your light so shine before men, that they may see your good works, and glorify your Father which is in heaven." By living truthfully, we become that light, helping others see the goodness of God and encouraging them to walk in His truth. Truthfulness gives us strength, reminding us that we don't have to go along with things that go against God's word. Instead, we can lovingly stand firm, showing others that following God's truth leads to a life of peace, joy, and purpose.

Being truthful also protects our hearts and minds. When we live in honesty and integrity, we don't have to carry the burden of lies or pretend to be something we're not. The Bible tells us in Psalm 51:6, "Behold, thou desirest truth in the inward parts: and in the hidden part thou shalt make me to know wisdom." God wants truth to be at the very core of who we are, shaping our thoughts, words, and actions. When we walk in truthfulness, we are free from the confusion and guilt that come from dishonesty. We are free to be who God made us to be, knowing that He loves us as we are. Truthfulness allows us to grow closer to God, as we are not hiding anything from Him or ourselves. This inner honesty brings peace, helping us to live with a clear conscience and a heart open to God's guidance.

On this trail from vision to mission, truthfulness also helps us be reliable witnesses for Christ. When others see that we are honest, that we live by our beliefs, and that we keep our promises, they are more likely to trust us and listen to our message. Our actions reflect God's truth, showing others that faith in Him is more than just words—it's a way of life. In a world where promises are often broken and commitments are easily discarded, our truthfulness can be a powerful example. Colossians 3:9 tells us, "Lie not one to another, seeing that ye have put off the old man with his deeds." This reminds us that as followers of Christ, we are called to be truthful, leaving behind dishonesty and living in the new life He has given us. By doing so, we show the world what it means to live for God, to honor Him in all that we do, and to be faithful representatives of His truth.

The journey from vision to mission is filled with opportunities to share God's love, and truthfulness is at the heart of it all. It helps us build meaningful relationships, where people feel safe, valued, and understood. It allows us to connect with others in a way that is real, showing them that God's love is authentic, unconditional, and unwavering. Truthfulness reminds us that God's truth is not something we have to change or hide to fit in with the world; instead, it is something we are called to live out boldly, with compassion and grace. By being truthful in love, we honor God and bring others closer to Him, showing them that His love is the foundation of everything we do. This trail from vision to mission teaches us that truthfulness is more than just telling the truth—it is living in a way that reflects God's character, a way that brings light, hope, and love to those around us. As we continue on this path, may we be committed to truthfulness in all we do, trusting that God will use our honesty, integrity, and love to make a difference in the world.

Chapter 7 – Teaching

The journey on the "Trail From Vision to Mission" includes a powerful calling to teach, a responsibility that comes when our hearts are moved with compassion for others. When we truly see the needs of people around us, both for hope and for understanding God's love, we are driven to share the truth of His Word with them. Jesus gave this mission to all His followers in Matthew 28:19, saying, "Go ye therefore, and teach all nations, baptizing them in the name of the Father, and of the Son, and of the Holy Ghost." This command shows us that teaching is an essential part of following Jesus, not just for pastors or leaders, but for every believer who has been touched by God's love. Teaching is more than just giving information; it's about helping others understand the truth of who God is, the depth of His love, and the hope He offers to everyone. Teaching means guiding others to see that God's Word is alive and relevant to their lives, offering wisdom, comfort, and direction. When we are moved with compassion, we want others to experience the peace, joy, and purpose we have found in knowing God. This desire fuels our mission to teach, to be a light for those who may feel lost or alone, and to help them see that God's love is real and available to them too.

Teaching on this journey involves patience and understanding, as we recognize that everyone is at a different place in their journey. Some may have never heard about God's love, while others may know but struggle to believe it applies to them. Compassionate teaching means meeting people where they are, taking the time to listen to their questions, and gently guiding them toward the truth. The Bible encourages us to teach with kindness and patience in 2 Timothy 2:24-25, "And the servant of the Lord must not strive; but be gentle unto all men, apt to teach, patient, in meekness instructing those that oppose themselves." This shows that teaching is not about arguing or forcing someone to believe, but rather showing love and respect as we share God's truth. Through compassionate teaching, we reflect God's character, making His message attractive and showing people that His ways are good. Our goal is not to win debates, but to open hearts, allowing others to see and feel God's love through us.

On the trail from vision to mission, teaching also involves setting an example through our actions. People learn from what we say, but they also learn from how we live. When our lives reflect the teachings of Christ, we become living examples of His love, kindness, and forgiveness. Jesus said in Matthew 5:16, "Let your light so shine before men, that they may see your good works, and glorify your Father which is in heaven." This means that teaching is not just about words, but about living in a way that shows God's goodness. When others see us treating people with kindness, forgiving those who have wronged us, and helping those in need, they begin to understand God's love in a deeper way. We teach by example, showing that following Jesus makes a real difference in how we live. Our actions speak volumes, and often, the way we live can open doors for conversations about faith, as people become curious about the hope and joy we carry.

Teaching also requires humility and a willingness to keep learning ourselves. As we teach others, we realize that we, too, are still learning and growing in our relationship with God. The Bible encourages us to seek wisdom in Proverbs 4:7, saying, "Wisdom is the principal thing; therefore get wisdom: and with all thy getting get understanding." This means that we should always be learning, growing in our understanding of God's Word so that we can teach others with wisdom and insight. A compassionate teacher knows that they don't have all the answers, but they are willing to walk alongside others, exploring God's truth together. This humility allows us to connect with people on a deeper level, as they see that we are not perfect, but we are sincerely trying to follow God's guidance. By being open and honest about our own journey, we make it easier for others to be open about theirs, creating a safe space for learning and growth.

The mission to teach also involves perseverance. Not everyone will understand or accept God's truth right away, and that can be discouraging. But teaching with compassion means that we continue to share, continue to love, and continue to offer God's hope, even when progress seems slow. Galatians 6:9 reminds us, "And let us not be weary in well doing: for in due season we shall reap, if we faint not." This verse encourages us to keep going, to trust that the seeds we are planting will grow in God's timing. Teaching is a long-term mission; it's about planting seeds of faith, hope, and love in people's hearts and trusting that God will bring growth. Sometimes, we may not see the results of our teaching immediately, but we can trust that God is working in ways we cannot see. Each act of kindness, each word of encouragement, and each moment we spend helping others understand God's love is a step on this journey from vision to mission, bringing us closer to fulfilling the purpose He has given us.

Teaching on this trail also involves helping others discover their own gifts and calling. As we share God's truth, we inspire others to see that they, too, have a place in His plan. Ephesians 2:10 tells us, "For we are his workmanship, created in Christ Jesus unto good works, which God hath before ordained that we should walk in them." This means that each person has a unique purpose, a calling from God to make a difference in the world. As we teach, we help people discover their own gifts, encouraging them to use those gifts to serve God and others. Teaching is about empowering others, giving them the tools and encouragement they need to grow in their faith and to step into the mission God has for them. When we teach with compassion, we are not just sharing information; we are building people up, helping them become who God created them to be. This is a beautiful part of the mission, as we watch others grow and begin to share God's love in their own unique ways.

In teaching, we are also reminded of the power of prayer. As we guide others on this journey, we realize that we need God's help every step of the way. Teaching is not something we can do on our own; we need God's wisdom, patience, and love to reach people's hearts. Philippians 4:6 encourages us to pray about everything, saying, "Be careful for nothing; but in every thing by prayer and supplication with thanksgiving let your requests be made known unto God." Prayer is an essential part of teaching, as we ask God to give us the right words, to soften hearts, and to work through us. Prayer connects us with God's power, reminding us that He is the one who changes hearts and brings understanding. As we pray, we trust that God will guide us, giving us opportunities to share His truth and helping us to be compassionate and effective teachers.

The trail from vision to mission, with a heart to teach, is ultimately a journey of love. We teach not out of obligation, but because we genuinely care about others and want them to experience the joy, peace, and purpose that come from knowing God. Teaching is an act of love, a way of reaching out to those who may feel lost, confused, or hopeless, and showing them that there is a path of light, guided by God's truth. 1 Corinthians 13:1 reminds us that without love, all our efforts are meaningless, saying, "Though I speak with the tongues of men and of angels, and have not charity, I am become as sounding brass, or a tinkling cymbal." This verse emphasizes that teaching, like everything else we do, must be rooted in love. When we teach with love, we reflect God's heart, showing people that they are valuable and that God's love is available to them.

Teaching on this journey from vision to mission also brings us closer to God, as we depend on Him for strength, guidance, and wisdom. Each time we teach, we are reminded of the truth we are sharing, and it strengthens our own faith. By teaching others, we ourselves grow deeper in our understanding of God's Word, as we learn to explain it clearly and to live it out in our own lives. This journey is one of mutual growth, where both the teacher and the learner draw closer to God. As we continue on this trail, teaching with compassion, patience, and love, we fulfill the mission Jesus gave us, spreading His truth and making a difference in the lives of those around us. May we always remember that teaching is a gift, a calling, and a beautiful part of our journey with God, as we bring His light and truth to the world.

Chapter 8 - Triumph Over Fear

The journey on the "Trail From Vision to Mission" calls us to triumph over fear, to stand boldly for Christ, and to walk in faith despite the challenges and doubts that may come our way. Fear is something that we all face at times, especially when we feel called to step out and do something that may be difficult, uncomfortable, or unknown. But God has given us a vision, a mission, and the strength to overcome fear and move forward with courage. In 2 Timothy 1:7, we are reminded, "For God hath not given us the spirit of fear; but of power, and of love, and of a sound mind." This powerful verse tells us that fear does not come from God; instead, He fills us with His strength, His love, and a clear, sound mind so that we can boldly follow His calling. When we have a vision of the mission God has set before us, it inspires us to overcome fear, knowing that we are not alone, and that He is with us every step of the way. We learn to trust that He has equipped us and will guide us, no matter how uncertain the path may seem. This mission gives us purpose, and with that purpose, we find the courage to face whatever may come.

As we walk on this trail, we learn that triumphing over fear is not about never feeling afraid, but about choosing to trust God even when fear tries to hold us back. Courage is not the absence of fear; it's the decision to move forward in spite of it. God knows our weaknesses, our insecurities, and our worries, yet He calls us to step out in faith, trusting that His strength is made perfect in our weakness (2 Corinthians 12:9). Each time we take a step of faith, we are reminded that God is greater than any fear we may face. He goes before us, preparing the way and giving us what we need to succeed. Fear may try to whisper lies, telling us that we are not good enough, strong enough, or brave enough. But God's truth speaks louder, reminding us that we are chosen, loved, and empowered by Him. Triumphing over fear means holding onto these truths, grounding ourselves in God's promises, and refusing to let fear dictate our actions.

One of the beautiful things about this journey from vision to mission is that, as we overcome fear, we grow stronger in our faith. Each step we take builds our trust in God, proving His faithfulness time and again. Fear begins to lose its grip as we see that God is with us, guiding us and providing for us in ways we could never have imagined. The Bible tells us in Psalm 27:1, "The Lord is my light and my salvation; whom shall I fear? the Lord is the strength of my life; of whom shall I be afraid?" This verse encourages us to find our strength and courage in God, knowing that with Him by our side, we have nothing to fear. He is our protector, our guide, and our source of strength. The more we rely on Him, the less power fear has over us. We begin to understand that fear is only as powerful as we allow it to be. When we keep our eyes on God and remember His promises, fear fades, and we are free to walk boldly in the purpose He has set before us.

Triumphing over fear also means realizing that the mission God has given us is greater than our own comfort. Sometimes, fear tries to keep us in a place of safety, where we don't have to take risks or step out of our comfort zones. But when we have a vision of the mission God has called us to, we understand that there is a greater purpose at stake. People are in need of hope, love, and the truth of God's Word, and He has chosen us to be vessels of that hope. This realization gives us the motivation to push past fear, knowing that what we are doing has eternal significance. Jesus Himself faced fear in the Garden of Gethsemane, yet He chose to move forward, saying, "Not my will, but thine, be done" (Luke 22:42). His love for us was greater than the fear of what lay ahead, and in His example, we find the strength to do the same. When we focus on the mission, on the lives that can be touched and transformed, fear loses its power, and we find ourselves willing to go wherever God leads.

On this journey, we also come to understand that God has given us the tools we need to overcome fear. He has given us His Word, filled with promises and encouragement, reminding us that He is always with us. He has given us the gift of prayer, a direct line to Him, where we can pour out our worries and receive His peace in return. Philippians 4:6-7 tells us, "Be careful for nothing; but in every thing by prayer and supplication with thanksgiving let your requests be made known unto God. And the peace of God, which passeth all understanding, shall keep your hearts and minds through Christ Jesus." This verse reminds us that we don't have to carry fear alone; we can bring it to God, and He will give us peace that goes beyond our understanding. Through prayer, we find the strength to keep going, knowing that God hears us and will answer.

Fear often tries to isolate us, making us feel like we are the only ones struggling or that no one else understands. But as we walk this trail, we realize that we are part of a community of believers, all striving to follow God's calling. We find strength in fellowship, in the support and encouragement of others who are also on this journey. Hebrews 10:24-25 encourages us, "And let us consider one another to provoke unto love and to good works: not forsaking the assembling of ourselves together." When we gather with others, share our fears, and pray for one another, we build each other up, making it easier to stand boldly for Christ. Together, we remind each other of God's promises, we celebrate victories, and we hold each other accountable, helping each other overcome the fears that try to hold us back.

As we continue on the trail from vision to mission, we learn that overcoming fear is a daily choice. It's not something we conquer once and for all, but something we face each day with renewed faith and trust in God. Some days may feel easier than others, but each day we choose to trust God is a victory. Each step we take strengthens our courage and deepens our faith. We begin to see that the things we once feared no longer have the same hold on us, because God has proven His faithfulness over and over. We learn to look back on His faithfulness as a source of strength, reminding ourselves of how far He has brought us and trusting that He will continue to lead us forward. Isaiah 41:10 gives us this encouragement: "Fear thou not; for I am with thee: be not dismayed; for I am thy God: I will strengthen thee; yea, I will help thee; yea, I will uphold thee with the right hand of my righteousness." This promise assures us that God will uphold us, giving us the strength to stand firm, no matter what challenges may come.

In the end, triumphing over fear on this journey from vision to mission is about surrendering our fears to God and letting His love fill us with courage. 1 John 4:18 says, "There is no fear in love; but perfect love casteth out fear." When we focus on God's love, fear has no place in our hearts. His love empowers us to go beyond our limitations, to reach out to those who need hope, and to stand boldly as witnesses for Christ. We are reminded that our mission is not about us, but about showing others the love and grace of God. Fear may try to hold us back, but God's love pushes us forward, giving us the strength to fulfill the calling He has placed on our lives.

So as we walk this trail, may we keep our eyes on the vision God has given us, trusting Him to guide us, empower us, and protect us. May we remember that we are not alone, that God's Spirit is within us, giving us the power to stand boldly and walk in faith. Triumphing over fear is not an easy journey, but it is a journey worth taking, one that brings us closer to God and allows us to fulfill the purpose He has created us for. With each step, we grow stronger, more confident, and more ready to share God's love with a world in need. This is the heart of our mission, to live boldly for Christ, overcoming fear, and shining His light for all to see.

Chapter 9 – Timeliness

The journey on the "Trail From Vision to Mission" teaches us the importance of timeliness, helping us to recognize the urgency of God's work and to commit to acting in His perfect timing. There is a need to understand that the work of God cannot be put off or delayed, for His mission is too important, and His timing is always right. In 2 Corinthians 6:2, the Bible reminds us, "For he saith, I have heard thee in a time accepted, and in the day of salvation have I succoured thee: behold, now is the accepted time; behold, now is the day of salvation." This verse calls us to see that God's timing is right now, that His call to serve and share His love with the world is urgent and should not be postponed. God has given each of us a purpose, a mission that is not only meant for someday, but for today, for each moment we have is an opportunity to make a difference in the lives of others. Timeliness on this trail means being sensitive to God's call and ready to respond whenever He leads, recognizing that there are people in need of His love, hope, and salvation right now. When we delay or put off what He has called us to do, we may miss out on the blessings He has for us and the opportunities to be a blessing to others. This sense of urgency does not mean rushing ahead without thought, but rather living with a sense of purpose and readiness, knowing that every moment we have is a gift from God that we can use to serve Him.

Timeliness in our mission means being aware of God's guidance and His timing in every situation. Sometimes, God may prompt us to speak to someone, to lend a hand, or to offer words of encouragement, and if we wait too long, the opportunity may pass. Acting in God's timing requires us to stay connected to Him, to pray, and to listen for His voice, allowing Him to direct our steps and show us when and where we are needed. In Ecclesiastes 3:1, it says, "To every thing there is a season, and a time to every purpose under the heaven." This reminds us that God has a plan for each moment, and by trusting in His timing, we find ourselves in the right place at the right time, ready to fulfill the purpose He has given us. Acting in God's timing also means trusting that He knows best, that even when we don't understand why or when He calls us to move, we can trust that His ways are higher than ours and that His timing is perfect. When we follow His lead, we find that things fall into place in ways we could not have planned ourselves, as He opens doors, provides opportunities, and leads us to people who need to see His love.

Being timely in God's mission also means understanding the needs of others and realizing that people often don't have time to wait. There are people around us who are hurting, who need comfort, hope, and the message of God's love today. By acting promptly, by reaching out in the moment we feel led, we can provide the support and love that they may not have found otherwise. Delaying our actions could mean someone misses the encouragement they need in a difficult time. James 4:17 tells us, "Therefore to him that knoweth to do good, and doeth it not, to him it is sin." This verse reminds us that when we know the right thing to do, when we know that God has placed an opportunity before us to serve, we are called to act. Timeliness in our mission is about taking the opportunities God gives us seriously, knowing that He has placed us where we are for a reason, to make a difference in the lives of those around us. Sometimes, we may feel hesitant or unsure, but trusting in God's timing gives us the courage to step out in faith, knowing that He has prepared the way for us.

Timeliness also means making the most of every moment, not waiting for a perfect time or place, but using each day to fulfill the mission God has given us. Ephesians 5:15-16 encourages us to, "See then that ye walk circumspectly, not as fools, but as wise, redeeming the time, because the days are evil." This verse calls us to be wise with our time, to value each day, and to recognize that we are living in a world that needs God's love and truth now more than ever. By walking in God's timing, by redeeming each moment, we make our lives count for His kingdom. This doesn't mean we have to be constantly busy, but it does mean living with purpose, being open to God's call in every situation, and being willing to serve whenever He leads. Timeliness on this trail means that we don't wait for tomorrow to live out God's purpose; we start today, knowing that each small act of kindness, each prayer, and each step we take in His name has eternal value.

On this journey from vision to mission, we also learn that timeliness includes trusting God's timing even when it's hard to wait. There will be times when God asks us to be patient, to wait for His perfect moment, and during these times, we may feel eager or anxious to move forward. Yet, God's timing is always right, and by waiting for His direction, we find that He prepares the way for us in ways we could not have done on our own. Isaiah 40:31 encourages us, "But they that wait upon the Lord shall renew their strength; they shall mount up with wings as eagles; they shall run, and not be weary; and they shall walk, and not faint." Waiting on God gives us strength and prepares us for what lies ahead. Sometimes, the delay is a time of growth, a time when God is working in our hearts, building our faith, and making us ready for the mission He has for us. Trusting in God's timing means being willing to wait when He says wait, and being ready to act when He says go. It is about aligning our lives with His plans, knowing that His ways are perfect, and that He sees the whole picture, while we see only a part.

Timeliness in God's work is also about being intentional, about setting aside distractions and focusing on what truly matters. In a world full of busyness and constant demands on our time, it can be easy to lose sight of our mission. But when we commit to following God's timing, we learn to prioritize the things that align with His purpose for our lives. We choose to invest our time in the things that bring us closer to Him and that help us to share His love with others. Colossians 4:5 tells us, "Walk in wisdom toward them that are without, redeeming the time." This reminds us to be wise in how we use our time, to make choices that reflect our commitment to God's mission. It means that we don't waste the precious moments we have, but we use them to build relationships, to serve, to pray, and to grow in our faith. By living in God's timing, we make our days meaningful, knowing that each moment we dedicate to Him is a step closer to fulfilling the vision He has given us.

Timeliness on this trail from vision to mission is ultimately about living with a sense of readiness, always prepared to respond to God's call, whether it's to reach out to someone in need, to share His Word, or to lend a helping hand. We understand that life is short, and the opportunities we have today may not come again. Psalm 90:12 reminds us, "So teach us to number our days, that we may apply our hearts unto wisdom." This verse encourages us to live wisely, to be aware of the time we have, and to use it for God's glory. As we walk this trail, we learn that timeliness is not just about doing things quickly, but about doing things with purpose, with love, and with a heart that is in tune with God. It is about being faithful in the small moments, knowing that God can use each one to make a difference.

In the end, recognizing the urgency of God's work and committing to act in His timing brings a deep sense of fulfillment. We find joy in knowing that we are part of something greater, that our lives are being used to bring hope and light to a world in need. As we stay sensitive to God's timing, we experience His presence in new and powerful ways, seeing His hand at work in every step we take. This journey from vision to mission is one of trust, faith, and obedience, where we learn to walk in step with God, ready to respond to His call at any moment. May we always be mindful of the time we have, and may we commit each day to serving Him with a heart that is open, a spirit that is willing, and a readiness to act in His perfect timing. This is the essence of our mission: to live fully for God, to use every moment for His glory, and to make a difference in the lives of those He places in our path.

Chapter 10 - Tuning In to God's Voice

The journey on the "Trail From Vision to Mission" teaches us the importance of tuning in to God's voice, listening to His guidance, and being willing to follow where He leads. Tuning in to God's voice is about more than just hearing Him; it's about being deeply connected to His will, understanding His heart, and allowing His words to affect our hearts and actions. When our hearts are affected by the love and compassion that God has for all people, we are more sensitive to His voice, and we become eager to serve those He places in our path. In Isaiah 6:8, the Bible says, "Also I heard the voice of the Lord, saying, Whom shall I send, and who will go for us? Then said I, Here am I; send me." This powerful response from Isaiah shows a willingness to listen and obey, a heart open to God's call, ready to go wherever He needs us. When we tune in to God's voice, we, too, find ourselves saying, "Here am I, send me." God's voice is not always loud; sometimes it is a gentle whisper, guiding us quietly, and we need to be still and attentive to hear it. In a world filled with noise, distractions, and countless demands on our attention, it's easy to miss God's voice if we're not intentional about listening. Tuning in requires us to pause, to spend time in prayer, to read His Word, and to be open to the Holy Spirit's promptings.

Listening to God's voice means letting go of our own plans and being willing to follow His direction, even when it may lead us somewhere unexpected. It requires humility, an understanding that God's ways are higher than our ways and His thoughts higher than our thoughts (Isaiah 55:8-9). When we trust that God knows best, we find the courage to step out in faith, knowing that He will guide us to the people who need Him most. Sometimes, tuning in to God's voice may lead us to help a stranger, to offer encouragement to a friend, or to share the message of hope with someone who feels lost. We may not always understand why God leads us to certain places or people, but by listening to His voice, we are part of His greater plan, a plan that reaches beyond what we can see. God's voice directs us, opening our eyes to see the needs of others, and filling our hearts with compassion. When we are in tune with Him, we are more aware of those who are hurting, lonely, or in need of encouragement. We become God's hands and feet, bringing His love, hope, and comfort to a world that desperately needs it.

Tuning in to God's voice also means recognizing that He speaks to us in many ways. God may speak through Scripture, through prayer, through the wise words of others, or even through circumstances in our lives. Each day, He gives us opportunities to hear Him, to learn from Him, and to draw closer to Him. Psalm 46:10 encourages us, "Be still, and know that I am God." This verse reminds us that sometimes we need to quiet our own thoughts, to step away from the busyness of life, and to simply listen. When we are still before God, we make room to hear His voice more clearly. God longs to speak to us, to guide us, and to help us grow, but we must be willing to listen. Tuning in to God's voice is about creating a habit of listening, making time each day to seek His guidance and to allow His words to shape our thoughts and actions. The more we listen, the more we understand His heart, and the easier it becomes to recognize His voice amid all the other voices around us.

This journey from vision to mission is also about tuning in to God's voice for direction, especially when we face challenges or uncertainty. There will be times when we don't know which path to take, when we feel unsure or even afraid. But when we are listening to God's voice, we find comfort and clarity, knowing that He will lead us. Proverbs 3:5-6 reminds us, "Trust in the Lord with all thine heart; and lean not unto thine own understanding. In all thy ways acknowledge him, and he shall direct thy paths." This verse encourages us to trust God completely, to lean on His wisdom rather than our own, and to acknowledge Him in all that we do. By tuning in to His voice, we open our hearts to His direction, and we find the courage to keep moving forward, even when the road ahead seems unclear. God's voice reassures us, reminding us that He is with us, that He has a purpose for us, and that He will not lead us astray.

Tuning in to God's voice also transforms our hearts, making us more compassionate, more loving, and more willing to serve. As we listen to Him, we begin to see people through His eyes, recognizing their value and their needs. God's voice calls us to love others deeply, to forgive, to show kindness, and

THE TRAIL FROM VISION TO MISSION

to reach out to those who are struggling. When we are in tune with God, we find that our hearts are softened, and we become more sensitive to the needs of others. The Bible tells us in Matthew 22:37-39, "Jesus said unto him, Thou shalt love the Lord thy God with all thy heart, and with all thy soul, and with all thy mind. This is the first and great commandment. And the second is like unto it, Thou shalt love thy neighbour as thyself." By listening to God's voice, we are reminded of these commandments, and we are inspired to live them out, loving God wholeheartedly and loving others as ourselves. God's voice leads us to put others before ourselves, to serve humbly, and to be a light in the lives of those around us.

On this journey, tuning in to God's voice also strengthens our faith. Each time we listen and obey, we see God's faithfulness in action, and our trust in Him grows. We begin to realize that He truly knows what is best, and this makes it easier to follow His guidance in the future. Tuning in to God's voice teaches us to rely on Him, to depend on His strength rather than our own, and to believe that He will provide for every need. Philippians 4:19 assures us, "But my God shall supply all your need according to his riches in glory by Christ Jesus." This verse reminds us that when we follow God's voice, we don't have to worry about how things will work out, for He will take care of us. Listening to God builds our confidence in Him, knowing that He is faithful and that He will not fail us.

Being in tune with God's voice on this trail from vision to mission is ultimately about being willing to go where He leads, to say "yes" to His call, and to trust that He will equip us for whatever He asks us to do. When we say, "Here am I; send me," we are stepping into a partnership with God, allowing Him to work through us to reach others. God's voice leads us to places we may not have chosen on our own, but when we follow, we find that He uses us in ways we never imagined. We become instruments of His love, bringing hope, joy, and healing to those who need it most. Each step we take in obedience to His voice brings us closer to fulfilling the mission He has given us. This journey from vision to mission is a journey of faith, trust, and surrender, where we learn to let go of our own plans and to embrace God's purpose for our lives.

Listening to God's voice also reminds us that we are never alone on this journey. He is always with us, guiding us, comforting us, and giving us the strength to keep going. Isaiah 41:10 encourages us, "Fear thou not; for I am with thee: be not dismayed; for I am thy God: I will strengthen thee; yea, I will help thee; yea, I will uphold thee with the right hand of my righteousness." This promise reassures us that no matter where God's voice leads us, He will be with us, providing everything we need. Tuning in to God's voice fills us with peace, knowing that we are following His plan and that He will never leave us. It is this assurance that gives us the courage to face challenges, to overcome obstacles, and to stay committed to the mission He has placed on our hearts.

In the end, tuning in to God's voice on the trail from vision to mission is about cultivating a deep, personal relationship with Him. It's about making time to listen, to pray, to read His Word, and to seek His guidance in all things. The more we listen, the more we recognize His voice, and the easier it becomes to follow where He leads. Tuning in to God's voice transforms our lives, filling us with purpose, direction, and a desire to make a difference in the world. It helps us to live with compassion, to serve with humility, and to love with a heart that reflects God's own love for humanity. As we walk this trail, may we continue to listen for His voice, to respond with willingness and faith, and to say, "Here am I; send me," ready to go wherever He calls and to fulfill the mission He has given us with joy, courage, and unwavering trust in His perfect plan.

Chapter 11 - Thirst for Righteousness

The journey on the "Trail From Vision to Mission" stirs in us a deep thirst for righteousness, a longing to see God's goodness, justice, and love fill our world. This thirst begins when we open our eyes and see the brokenness around us—the hurt, the injustice, the pain that so many people face. When we look at the world with God's eyes, we can't ignore the suffering we see; instead, our hearts ache, and we feel a deep desire to make things right. Jesus tells us in Matthew 5:6, "Blessed are they which do hunger and thirst after righteousness: for they shall be filled." This verse promises that those who long for righteousness, who want to see goodness and justice, will be satisfied. God honors this thirst, because it reflects His own heart; He is a God of justice, mercy, and truth, and He calls us to care deeply about these things as well. This longing for righteousness drives us forward on the path from vision to mission, giving us purpose and determination to act, to make a difference, and to bring light to the darkness we see in the world. When we thirst for righteousness, we're not just wishing for things to be better; we are moved to take steps that align with God's vision, to be His hands and feet, and to share His love with those who need it most.

This thirst for righteousness means that we want to see God's standards upheld, to see truth and honesty valued, to see kindness and compassion shown to all people. When we look around and see dishonesty, hatred, and injustice, it stirs something in our souls that tells us things should not be this way. This is because God created the world to be a place of peace, love, and fairness, and though sin has brought brokenness, our desire for righteousness connects us to God's original design. We long for a world where people treat each other with respect, where the weak are protected, where the hungry are fed, and where everyone has a chance to live a life full of hope and love. This longing is not something we can ignore; it grows within us and becomes a driving force that propels us on the mission God has given us. We understand that we are part of God's plan to bring His justice and mercy to the world, to act as His agents of change, and to spread His light in places that desperately need it.

This thirst also helps us become more aware of our own need for righteousness, urging us to grow closer to God and to live according to His ways. We realize that before we can bring righteousness to the world, we must first seek it in our own lives. We start by asking God to cleanse our hearts, to guide us in His truth, and to help us live lives that reflect His goodness. Psalm 51:10 says, "Create in me a clean heart, O God; and renew a right spirit within me." This verse reminds us that righteousness begins within, as we ask God to shape us, to remove any bitterness or selfishness, and to fill us with His love and compassion. By seeking righteousness in our own lives, we become examples of God's love, showing others what it looks like to live in His light. This personal transformation is a crucial step on the journey from vision to mission, because it prepares us to serve others with pure motives and a heart full of God's love. When people see the change in us, they may be inspired to seek God for themselves, knowing that He is the source of all that is good, just, and true.

The thirst for righteousness also brings us closer to those who are suffering, those who feel alone, oppressed, or forgotten. This desire to see justice compels us to reach out, to stand with those who are struggling, and to be a voice for those who cannot speak for themselves. Proverbs 31:8-9 urges us, "Open thy mouth for the dumb in the cause of all such as are appointed to destruction. Open thy mouth, judge righteously, and plead the cause of the poor and needy." These verses remind us that God calls us to speak up, to defend those who are vulnerable, and to fight for what is right. This mission is not always easy, and it may require courage, sacrifice, and even facing opposition. Yet, when we thirst for righteousness, we find the strength to persevere, knowing that we are not alone. God is with us, guiding us, and giving us the wisdom and courage to make a difference. We don't have to be perfect or have all the answers; we simply need a heart that is willing, a spirit that is compassionate, and a desire to see God's justice come to life.

On this journey, we learn that righteousness and justice are not just about big, dramatic actions; they are also about the small, everyday choices we make. It's in the way we treat others with respect, in how we stand up for someone who is being mistreated, in how we choose honesty over deception, and in how we show kindness to those who are often overlooked. Each small act of righteousness reflects God's heart and brings His light into the world. Micah 6:8 reminds us of what God requires from us, saying, "He hath shewed thee, O man, what is good; and what doth the Lord require of thee, but to do justly, and to love mercy, and to walk humbly with thy God?" This verse shows that righteousness is not just about grand gestures; it is about living a life that honors God in all things, showing mercy, acting justly, and staying humble before Him. Each of these actions, though small on their own, adds up to create a ripple effect that touches the lives of others and brings them closer to God's love.

The thirst for righteousness also strengthens our faith, as we learn to rely on God's power to bring change, knowing that He is the ultimate source of justice. There will be times when the task seems overwhelming, when the problems of the world feel too big, and when we feel like our efforts are not making a difference. But in those moments, we turn to God, trusting that He is in control and that He will work through us in ways we may not see or understand. Isaiah 41:10 encourages us, "Fear thou not; for I am with thee: be not dismayed; for I am thy God: I will strengthen thee; yea, I will help thee; yea, I will uphold thee with the right hand of my righteousness." This promise reminds us that we don't have to bring about justice on our own; God is our strength, and He will help us every step of the way. Our thirst for righteousness drives us to pray, to seek God's guidance, and to trust in His power to bring change, even in the most difficult situations. We realize that true righteousness comes from Him, and that as we align our hearts with His, we become instruments of His love and justice in the world.

As we continue on this trail from vision to mission, our thirst for righteousness grows, deepening our commitment to live out God's love in tangible ways. This longing for justice keeps us focused, reminding us of why we are here and the impact we can have when we follow God's call. We are not content to sit back and watch from the sidelines; we are moved to action, to be a part of God's work in bringing healing, hope, and justice to a hurting world. We understand that our mission is not just for today but for the future, that the seeds of righteousness we plant now will continue to grow, touching lives and changing hearts long after we are gone. Each step we take on this path brings us closer to fulfilling the vision God has placed in our hearts, and we find joy in knowing that we are part of His greater plan.

Ultimately, the thirst for righteousness on the trail from vision to mission is about bringing God's kingdom to earth, sharing His love, and living in a way that reflects His heart. It's about showing others that there is a better way, a way of love, compassion, and justice. We are reminded of the prayer Jesus taught us in Matthew 6:10, "Thy kingdom come, Thy will be done in earth, as it is in heaven." This prayer expresses our desire to see God's will done, to see His righteousness fill the world, and to be part of that mission. As we walk this trail, may we never lose our thirst for righteousness, may we continue to seek God's guidance, and may we be willing to step out in faith, knowing that He is with us and that His love and justice will prevail. This is our mission, our calling, and our joy, to live each day for Him, bringing His light, hope, and righteousness to a world in need.

Chapter 12 – Tenderheartedness

The journey on the "Trail From Vision to Mission" fills us with a spirit of tenderheartedness, softening our hearts and drawing us closer to the love and mercy of Christ. Tenderheartedness means having a heart that is sensitive, compassionate, and ready to show kindness to others, no matter their situation. Colossians 3:12 reminds us, "Put on therefore, as the elect of God, holy and beloved, bowels of mercies, kindness, humbleness of mind, meekness, longsuffering." This verse calls us to clothe ourselves in qualities that reflect Jesus' heart—merciful, kind, humble, gentle, and patient. As we walk this path, our vision of God's love and the needs of the world stirs us to be tenderhearted, to let go of harshness, and to treat others with the grace and forgiveness that Christ has shown to us. When our hearts are softened, we are better able to see people through God's eyes, understanding that each person we meet has struggles, hopes, and needs just like us. We become less quick to judge and more willing to lend a helping hand or offer a comforting word. Tenderheartedness draws us into a life of compassion, where we genuinely care about the welfare of others, especially those who are hurting, lonely, or lost. It's more than just feeling sorry for others; it's a deep empathy that compels us to act, to reach out with kindness and to show others that they are loved by God.

Tenderheartedness on this trail means being willing to forgive and to let go of grudges, just as Christ forgave us. We understand that none of us are perfect, that we all make mistakes, and that we all need grace. When our hearts are tender, we are able to forgive more easily, knowing that holding onto bitterness only hardens our hearts and creates barriers between us and others. Ephesians 4:32 encourages us, "And be ye kind one to another, tenderhearted, forgiving one another, even as God for Christ's sake hath forgiven you." Forgiveness is a powerful act of tenderness, a way to release anger and choose love over resentment. As we forgive, we experience freedom, and we open the door for healing and reconciliation. Forgiving others doesn't mean we forget the pain, but it allows us to move forward, to let go of the burden of anger, and to fill our hearts with compassion instead. Tenderheartedness reminds us that everyone is in need of God's mercy, including ourselves, and this humility enables us to approach others with understanding and kindness.

This journey of tenderheartedness also brings us closer to Jesus, who was the ultimate example of compassion and mercy. Throughout His life, Jesus showed tenderheartedness to everyone He met, healing the sick, comforting the brokenhearted, and forgiving those who had wronged Him. His heart was always open to those in need, and He never turned away anyone who sought His help. When we strive to be like Christ, our hearts become more compassionate, and we find ourselves reaching out to those who are often overlooked or forgotten. In Matthew 9:36, we see Jesus' compassion as He looked at the crowds: "But when he saw the multitudes, he was moved with compassion on them, because they fainted, and were scattered abroad, as sheep having no shepherd." This verse shows us the depth of Jesus' tenderheartedness, His genuine concern for those who were lost and in need. When we allow ourselves to be moved by the needs of others, we begin to share in Christ's compassion, and our mission becomes clear—to love and serve others as He did.

Tenderheartedness also makes us more patient and understanding, recognizing that everyone has their own battles and that change takes time. When we encounter people who may be difficult or who may not respond to kindness right away, a tender heart reminds us to be patient, to keep loving, and to trust that God is working in their lives. Colossians 3:12 reminds us to put on "longsuffering," which is a gentle way of saying patience and endurance in dealing with others. This patience is a form of tenderness, showing that we are willing to walk alongside others, offering support and encouragement without giving up on them. Tenderheartedness is not about expecting immediate results; it's about faithfully showing love, knowing that even small acts of kindness can make a big difference over time. By being patient, we reflect God's own patience with us, His willingness to guide us, and His understanding of our own struggles.

As we continue on this trail, tenderheartedness opens our eyes to the beauty of serving others. When we serve with a tender heart, we do not serve out of obligation or for recognition; we serve because we genuinely care about others. We find joy in helping, in lifting others up, and in bringing a smile to someone's face. Acts of service, when done with a tender heart, become acts of love, reflecting God's care for each person we encounter. Jesus Himself demonstrated this in John 13:14-15, when He washed His disciples' feet, saying, "If I then, your Lord and Master, have washed your feet; ye also ought to wash one another's feet. For I have given you an example, that ye should do as I have done to you." This act of humility and service shows us that true greatness is found in serving others, in being willing to put their needs before our own. Tenderheartedness invites us to follow Jesus' example, to serve with humility, and to find joy in being a blessing to others.

This journey also teaches us that tenderheartedness is a strength, not a weakness. In a world that often values toughness, power, and self-reliance, it can be easy to think that tenderness makes us vulnerable. But in reality, a tender heart is a strong heart, one that is open, resilient, and full of love. It takes courage to be compassionate, to put others' needs before our own, and to care deeply about people. Tenderheartedness makes us stronger because it connects us to God's love, a love that never fails and that overcomes all things. Proverbs 4:23 tells us, "Keep thy heart with all diligence; for out of it are the issues of life." This verse reminds us that our hearts are precious, that they guide our actions and our interactions with others. By keeping our hearts tender, we allow God's love to flow through us, impacting others in ways we may not even realize.

On this trail from vision to mission, tenderheartedness becomes the foundation of our purpose, the reason we reach out, and the fuel that keeps us going. It gives us a deeper sense of empathy, helping us to connect with others on a personal level, to share in their joys and sorrows, and to offer a listening ear and a compassionate heart. When we have a tender heart, we don't just see people's outward circumstances; we feel their struggles, their hopes, and their dreams. We become more aware of the challenges others face, and we are moved to help in whatever ways we can, whether through prayer, encouragement, or acts of kindness. Tenderheartedness reminds us that we are all connected, that we are all part of God's family, and that we have a responsibility to care for one another.

Ultimately, tenderheartedness on this journey is about living out the love of Christ in everything we do. It's about being a reflection of His kindness, His forgiveness, and His compassion. When we are tenderhearted, we make room for God's love to work through us, bringing hope and healing to a world that desperately needs it. Our mission becomes not just about words, but about actions that show God's love in real, tangible ways. Each act of kindness, each moment of patience, and each gesture of compassion brings us closer to fulfilling the vision God has placed in our hearts. Tenderheartedness transforms us, shaping us to be more like Christ and helping us to be His hands and feet in a world that is often hurting and in need of love.

As we walk this trail, may we continue to cultivate a tender heart, open to God's love and ready to share it with others. May we always remember that true strength is found in kindness, that real courage is shown in compassion, and that lasting impact is made through love. This journey from vision to mission is a journey of the heart, a path that leads us closer to God and helps us to bring His light into the lives of those around us. May our tenderheartedness be a testimony of God's grace, a reflection of His mercy, and a reminder of His never-ending love for all people. This is our calling, our purpose, and our joy—to walk this trail with tender hearts, to serve with compassion, and to fulfill the mission of love that God has given us.

Chapter 13 - Taking Initiative

The journey on the "Trail From Vision to Mission" calls us to take initiative in sharing God's love, a powerful step that happens when our hearts are moved by His vision and filled with a desire to serve others. Taking initiative means we don't just wait around for the perfect moment or for someone else to step up; instead, we willingly respond to God's call, choosing to act with purpose, compassion, and courage. In Acts 10:34-35, we see Peter declaring, "Of a truth I perceive that God is no respecter of persons: But in every nation he that feareth him, and worketh righteousness, is accepted with him." This passage reveals that God's love and salvation are for everyone, and because of this, we are called to share His love with all people, without hesitation or discrimination. When our hearts are touched by God's vision for the world, we feel a deep responsibility to make His love known to others, taking initiative to reach out, to serve, and to show kindness in His name. Taking initiative is not about seeking recognition or praise; it's about stepping forward because we know that God's love is too wonderful to keep to ourselves. We are inspired to take that first step, to open a door, or to start a conversation that may bring someone closer to knowing God's love. This mission is about being proactive, looking for opportunities to help, and being willing to go out of our way to make a difference. When we take initiative, we become vessels of God's grace, spreading His light in places that may have never experienced it before.

Taking initiative on this trail means listening to God's guidance and being ready to act whenever and wherever He leads us. Sometimes, this may mean reaching out to a stranger who looks downcast, offering a helping hand to someone in need, or speaking words of encouragement to a friend who is struggling. These acts don't have to be big or grand; they just need to come from a genuine place of love and a willingness to serve. Every small step we take to show kindness and compassion matters, and God can use even the simplest actions to make a profound impact in someone's life. James 1:22 encourages us, "But be ye doers of the word, and not hearers only, deceiving your own selves." This verse reminds us that our faith must be active, that we are called not only to hear God's Word but to live it out through our actions. Taking initiative is an expression of our faith in action, a way to put God's love into practice, and a testament to the transformation He has worked in our hearts. When we actively seek ways to help others, we reflect the love of Christ, showing them that they are valued, loved, and not forgotten.

Initiative on this mission also means being courageous, willing to step out of our comfort zones to serve others. Sometimes, taking initiative might involve doing something that feels uncomfortable or challenging. We may be called to reach out to people we don't know well, to go to places we haven't been, or to offer help in situations that seem beyond our ability. But when our hearts are moved by God's vision, we trust that He will give us the courage and strength to do what He has asked. Philippians 4:13 reminds us, "I can do all things through Christ which strengtheneth me." This verse assures us that with God's help, we can overcome any fear, hesitation, or uncertainty, and boldly take the steps He calls us to take. Taking initiative means placing our trust in God, knowing that He will equip us for the task and that He will be with us every step of the way. Each time we step out in faith, we grow stronger, more confident in our calling, and more aware of God's presence in our lives.

On this trail, taking initiative also means being willing to take the lead in situations where we see a need. Sometimes, we may find ourselves in situations where others are unsure of what to do or are hesitant to take action. In these moments, God may be calling us to step forward, to offer a solution, or to encourage others to get involved. Taking initiative means we don't wait for someone else to start; instead, we become the ones who start, showing others the way through our example. Jesus showed this kind of leadership and initiative throughout His life. He didn't wait for others to take action; He saw the needs around Him, and He met them with compassion and love. When He saw the hungry, He fed them; when He saw the sick, He healed them; and when He saw the lost, He reached out to them. Following Jesus' example, we learn that taking initiative is about being ready to serve, to lead with love, and to show others what it means to live out God's vision.

Taking initiative also requires us to be attentive and open to the needs of others. It's easy to become wrapped up in our own lives, focused on our own concerns, but a heart moved by God's vision is always on the lookout for ways to help. We begin to see people through God's eyes, noticing when someone is hurting, lonely, or in need of support. Instead of passing by, we feel compelled to do something, to offer a listening ear, a comforting word, or a helping hand. Galatians 6:2 encourages us, "Bear ye one another's burdens, and so fulfil the law of Christ." This verse reminds us that taking initiative is not just about doing things for ourselves but about carrying each other's burdens and sharing in each other's struggles. When we take initiative, we become part of the solution, showing others that they are not alone and that God's love is present, even in the hardest of times.

Initiative on this trail also teaches us to be persistent, to keep going even when things don't go as planned. There may be times when our efforts don't seem to make a difference, when the people we try to help are unresponsive, or when we face obstacles that make it hard to keep moving forward. But taking initiative means we don't give up; we continue to serve, trusting that God is working through us, even if we can't see the results right away. Galatians 6:9 encourages us, "And let us not be weary in well doing: for in due season we shall reap, if we faint not." This verse reminds us to stay strong, to keep taking steps forward, knowing that our work is not in vain. Every act of kindness, every moment of service, and every word of encouragement is a seed planted in someone's life, and God will bring growth in His timing. By taking initiative and staying committed, we become a source of hope and strength for others, a reminder that God's love is unwavering and that He is always working for good.

Taking initiative also allows us to grow in our own faith, as each step we take teaches us to rely on God and to trust His plan. When we take the first step in serving others, we are often stretched in ways we didn't expect. We may face challenges, but through these experiences, we learn to lean on God's strength and to grow in wisdom and compassion. Taking initiative becomes a journey of faith, a path that deepens our relationship with God as we see Him work in and through us. We start to realize that every act of service, no matter how small, is significant in God's eyes and that He uses each step we take to shape us into people who reflect His love. In Matthew 5:16, Jesus says, "Let your light so shine before men, that they may see your good works, and glorify your Father which is in heaven." This verse reminds us that our acts of initiative are a way to let God's light shine through us, to show the world who He is and to bring glory to His name.

Ultimately, taking initiative on the trail from vision to mission is about living with a heart that is fully committed to God's purpose. It's about being willing to say, "Here I am, Lord, use me," and then stepping out in faith, trusting that He will guide us. When we take initiative, we become active participants in God's mission, people who are ready to share His love wherever we go. This journey teaches us that taking initiative is not about perfection; it's about a willingness to act, a readiness to serve, and a heart that is open to God's leading. Each time we step forward, we bring a little more of God's kingdom to earth, making a difference in the lives of those around us and fulfilling the vision He has given us. Taking initiative transforms us, fills us with purpose, and brings us closer to God as we partner with Him in His work. This is our calling, our joy, and our mission—to take the first step, to reach out with love, and to be instruments of God's grace in a world that needs His light more than ever.

Chapter 14 – Trustworthiness

The journey on the "Trail From Vision to Mission" teaches us the importance of trustworthiness, showing us that when our hearts align with God's will and purpose, we become trustworthy stewards of His message. To be trustworthy means that people can rely on us to be truthful, dependable, and faithful in what we say and do. Trustworthiness is a quality that grows within us as we draw closer to God, listening to His Word and following His ways. In 1 Corinthians 4:2, we read, "Moreover it is required in stewards, that a man be found faithful." This verse reminds us that as stewards of God's message, we are called to be faithful—to handle His truth with respect, honesty, and care. God entrusts us with the responsibility to share His love, His teachings, and His hope with others, and we honor this trust by being committed to Him and to the mission He has given us. Being trustworthy in God's eyes means living in a way that reflects His goodness, showing others that we are sincere in our faith, that we live what we believe, and that we can be relied upon to uphold His truth. Trustworthiness is not just about saying the right things; it's about letting our actions, our decisions, and our character be shaped by God's love and truth. When people see that we are trustworthy, they are more likely to listen to the message of hope we bring, knowing that we are genuine in our desire to share God's love.

Trustworthiness on this trail means being honest in all things, big and small, because we know that even the smallest actions reflect who we are and what we believe. We don't make promises lightly, and we keep our word, because we understand that our words carry weight. Trustworthiness means that others can count on us to follow through, to be people who don't just talk about God's love, but who live it every day. The Bible calls us to let our "yea be yea; and [our] nay, nay" (Matthew 5:37), reminding us that our words should be truthful and straightforward, without any deception or hidden motives.

When we speak truthfully and live with integrity, we build trust, showing others that we are people of our word. This reliability creates a foundation for sharing God's message, as people are more open to hearing from someone they can trust. Trustworthiness is a bridge that connects us to others, opening the door for genuine relationships where God's truth can be shared in a way that touches hearts and changes lives.

Being trustworthy also means handling God's message with care, ensuring that we share it accurately and respectfully. God's truth is powerful, and it is not something to be used for our own gain or to impress others. We are stewards of His message, which means we have a responsibility to present it honestly, without adding our own opinions or twisting it to fit our desires. 2 Timothy 2:15 encourages us to "study to shew thyself approved unto God, a workman that needeth not to be ashamed, rightly dividing the word of truth." This verse reminds us that we must approach God's Word with humility and diligence, seeking to understand it fully so that we can share it faithfully. Trustworthiness requires us to be careful and thoughtful, to study God's Word, and to ask for His guidance as we share it with others. When people see that we are committed to truth, that we don't change God's message to suit our own needs, they can trust that what we share is real, honest, and life-giving.

On this journey from vision to mission, trustworthiness also means being consistent in our actions, showing that our faith is not just something we talk about, but something we live out daily. Consistency builds trust because it shows that our commitment to God's mission is steady and sincere. We don't live one way in public and another way in private; instead, we seek to let God's love and truth shine through in every part of our lives. This consistency is a form of integrity, where we strive to be the same person wherever we are, letting our lives be a true reflection of God's goodness. James 1:22 says, "But be ye doers of the word, and not hearers only, deceiving your own selves." This verse reminds us that it's not enough to simply know God's truth; we must also live it. By putting God's Word into action, we show others that we are serious about our faith, that we are committed to following Jesus, and that we can be trusted to share His love honestly and faithfully.

Trustworthiness also involves being dependable, being someone who others can rely on when they need help, support, or encouragement. We show up for others, we stand by them in times of trouble, and we are there to offer a listening ear, a comforting word, or a helping hand. In Galatians 6:2, we are encouraged to "Bear ye one another's burdens, and so fulfil the law of Christ." This verse calls us to support each other, to be there for others as Christ is there for us. When we are dependable, we become a source of strength for those around us, someone they can turn to when they feel alone or uncertain. Our trustworthiness creates a safe space for others, allowing them to feel comfortable sharing their struggles, knowing that we will respond with love and compassion. By being dependable, we show others that God's love is steadfast, that He is always there for us, and that they can rely on Him just as they can rely on us.

Being trustworthy also requires humility, recognizing that our ability to be trustworthy stewards of God's message comes from Him. We are not perfect, and we may make mistakes along the way, but when we walk humbly with God, we allow Him to guide us and correct us. Proverbs 3:5-6 reminds us to "Trust in the Lord with all thine heart; and lean not unto thine own understanding. In all thy ways acknowledge him, and he shall direct thy paths." This verse encourages us to rely on God's wisdom, to seek His guidance, and to trust that He will help us stay on the right path. Trustworthiness grows in us as we surrender our lives to God, letting Him shape us and lead us. When we are humble before God, we become more sensitive to His guidance, more willing to learn, and more open to correction. This humility helps us to stay true to His mission, to avoid pride, and to remember that our strength comes from Him alone.

Trustworthiness on this trail also means being faithful in the small things, understanding that every action, no matter how small, is important in God's eyes. Luke 16:10 tells us, "He that is faithful in that which is least is faithful also in much." This verse reminds us that trustworthiness begins with being faithful in the little things, in the everyday moments where we choose to act with integrity, kindness, and honesty. Whether it's keeping a promise, helping someone in need, or being honest in our words, each small act builds trust and shows our commitment to God's mission. When we are faithful in the small things, God entrusts us with greater responsibilities, knowing that we will handle them with care. Each step we take on this path, each choice to be honest, each moment of kindness, brings us closer to fulfilling the vision God has placed in our hearts.

Ultimately, trustworthiness on the trail from vision to mission is about being a faithful reflection of God's character. As we grow in trustworthiness, we become more like Christ, who is the ultimate example of faithfulness, honesty, and integrity. Jesus never broke a promise, never spoke falsely, and never turned away from those in need. He was trustworthy in every way, and as we follow His example, we learn to be trustworthy stewards of His message. Our mission is to share His love and truth with a world that desperately needs it, and by living with trustworthiness, we make His love real and tangible for those around us. We become a living testimony of His grace, showing others that they can trust in Him because He is faithful, and His love never fails. This journey from vision to mission is a path of trust, where we learn to rely on God, to be faithful in all things, and to let His light shine through us as trustworthy stewards of His message. This is our calling, our joy, and our mission—to walk in trustworthiness, to honor God in all we do, and to share His love with a world in need of hope.

Chapter 15 - Total Surrender

The journey on the "Trail From Vision to Mission" calls us to total surrender, to give our whole selves to God's purpose and trust Him to lead us every step of the way. Total surrender means we let go of our own plans, desires, and fears, and we place our lives fully in God's hands, allowing Him to guide our journey. In Galatians 2:20, Paul says, "I am crucified with Christ: nevertheless I live; yet not I, but Christ liveth in me: and the life which I now live in the flesh I live by the faith of the Son of God, who loved me, and gave himself for me." This verse reminds us that when we surrender to God, we live a life that is no longer centered around ourselves but around Christ, who lives in us and works through us. When we truly understand God's vision for us—His love, His mercy, and His calling—we find the courage to let go and trust Him completely. Total surrender doesn't mean we lose ourselves; instead, we find our true purpose, because we are living for something greater than ourselves. We are living for God's mission, a mission that is filled with meaning, love, and hope. This surrender leads us to give everything we have—our time, our energy, our talents, and our resources—to serve God and to help others, knowing that He will guide us and provide for us along the way.

Surrendering fully to God means saying, "Not my will, but Thine be done" (Luke 22:42), as Jesus did. It's a choice to trust that God knows what's best for us, even when His plan is different from ours. Sometimes, surrender means letting go of our dreams or stepping out of our comfort zones, but we can be assured that God's plan for us is filled with purpose and love. He sees the bigger picture, and when we surrender, we are saying, "God, I trust that Your way is better than mine." This act of trust frees us from the pressure of trying to control everything, because we know that God is in control. We can have peace, knowing that He will lead us exactly where we need to be. When we let go of our own plans, we make room for God to work in powerful ways, opening doors and creating opportunities we could never have imagined on our own. Total surrender allows us to walk forward in faith, even when we can't see the whole path, knowing that God will reveal each step as we go.

This path of total surrender also brings us closer to God, helping us to rely on Him and to grow in our relationship with Him. When we surrender, we become more sensitive to God's voice, more willing to follow His guidance, and more open to His presence in our lives. In Proverbs 3:5-6, the Bible encourages us, "Trust in the Lord with all thine heart; and lean not unto thine own understanding. In all thy ways acknowledge him, and he shall direct thy paths." This verse reminds us that when we surrender fully, when we trust God with all our hearts, He will lead us on the right path. We don't have to understand everything; we just need to trust that God does. Total surrender is about letting go of our need for answers and choosing to follow, even when we don't know where the road will lead. It's about saying, "God, I trust You to take me where I need to go, and I will follow wherever You lead." Each step we take in surrender brings us closer to God, deepening our faith and helping us to experience His love and peace in new ways.

On this trail from vision to mission, total surrender also means allowing God to use us in whatever way He chooses. We no longer hold back, afraid of what might happen or worried about what others might think. Instead, we are fully committed, willing to serve, to speak, and to give as God leads. We understand that our lives are not our own, but belong to God, who has a purpose for each of us. Romans 12:1 urges us, "I beseech you therefore, brethren, by the mercies of God, that ye present your bodies a living sacrifice, holy, acceptable unto God, which is your reasonable service." This verse calls us to offer ourselves completely to God, to live as a sacrifice, dedicated to His work and open to His call. Total surrender means we hold nothing back, but we give our whole selves to God's mission, trusting that He will use us for His glory. It's a way of living that says, "God, here I am. Use me as You will." This willingness to be used by God transforms us, shaping us to be more like Jesus, who surrendered His life to serve, to love, and to save.

Total surrender also teaches us humility, helping us to recognize that we need God's strength and wisdom in every part of our mission. We cannot fulfill God's vision on our own; we need His guidance, His power, and His love working through us. Surrendering to God means admitting our weaknesses and asking for His help, trusting that His strength is made perfect in our weakness (2 Corinthians 12:9). When we let go of our pride and our desire to do things our way, we make room for God to do great things in and through us. Total surrender is a posture of humility, a heart that says, "God, I can't do this without You, but I trust that You will give me the strength I need." As we humble ourselves, God lifts us up, giving us the courage and the grace to carry out His mission.

On this journey, total surrender also means being willing to serve others, to put their needs before our own, and to love them with the love of Christ. When we surrender to God's mission, we realize that our purpose is not just about us, but about reaching out to those who need to know God's love. Philippians 2:3-4 encourages us, "Let nothing be done through strife or vainglory; but in lowliness of mind let each esteem other better than themselves. Look not every man on his own things, but every man also on the things of others." This verse reminds us that surrender is about selflessness, about caring for others and putting their needs first. When we are fully surrendered to God's mission, we see others with compassion, and we are willing to serve them in whatever way we can. Total surrender opens our hearts to be used by God to make a difference, to bring hope, and to share His love with those who are hurting, lost, or in need.

Surrendering to God's mission also means letting go of our fears and trusting that He will take care of us. There may be times when following God's call feels risky, when we are asked to step into the unknown or to face challenges that seem overwhelming. But total surrender means we trust that God is with us, that He will protect us, and that He will provide for every need. Isaiah 41:10 encourages us, "Fear thou not; for I am with thee: be not dismayed; for I am thy God: I will strengthen thee; yea, I will help thee; yea, I will uphold thee with the right hand of my righteousness." This promise reminds us that we are not alone, that God is with us every step of the way. When we surrender fully, we find peace, knowing that God is our protector, our provider, and our strength. We don't have to worry about the future, because we know that God holds it in His hands.

Ultimately, total surrender on the trail from vision to mission is about giving our lives completely to God, trusting that He will use us for His purpose and for His glory. It's a journey of faith, a path that leads us closer to God and helps us to experience His love and presence in a deeper way. When we surrender fully, we discover the joy of living for something greater than ourselves, of being part of God's work in the world, and of making a difference in the lives of others. Each step of surrender brings us closer to fulfilling the vision God has placed in our hearts, allowing us to live a life filled with purpose, love, and hope. May we walk this trail with open hearts, willing to let go, to trust, and to follow wherever God leads. This is the heart of our mission—to live in total surrender to God, letting Him guide our steps, and sharing His love with a world that needs it more than ever. This is our calling, our purpose, and our joy, to walk in surrender, to trust in God's plan, and to fulfill the mission He has given us.

Chapter 16 - Triumphant Spirit

The journey on the "Trail From Vision to Mission" fills us with a triumphant spirit, a deep sense of victory and hope that comes from knowing we are part of God's Kingdom. This triumphant spirit is not rooted in our own abilities or successes but in the unshakeable truth that God is with us and has already secured the ultimate victory. In Romans 8:37, the Bible declares, "Nay, in all these things we are more than conquerors through him that loved us." This verse reminds us that because of God's love, we can face any challenge, any hardship, and any fear with a heart full of courage and strength. Being "more than conquerors" means that through Christ, we don't just overcome obstacles; we rise above them with confidence, knowing that God's power is at work within us. As we follow the vision He has given us, this triumphant spirit fuels our passion and our purpose, enabling us to keep moving forward even when the path is difficult. God's promise of victory gives us hope, reminding us that no matter how dark the world may seem, His light shines brighter, and His love is stronger. We know that every step we take on this mission is part of God's grand design, and this fills us with a joy that cannot be taken away.

A triumphant spirit on this trail also gives us resilience, the ability to keep going no matter what challenges arise. Life's journey is not without trials; we may face opposition, setbacks, or even moments of doubt. But when our spirit is rooted in the hope of God's Kingdom, we find the strength to persevere. We don't give up, because we know that God is working through every challenge, shaping us and growing us in ways we might not understand right away. James 1:2-4 encourages us, "My brethren, count it all joy when ye fall into divers temptations; Knowing this, that the trying of your faith worketh patience. But let patience have her perfect work, that ye may be perfect and entire, wanting nothing." This passage reminds us that the struggles we face are part of God's refining process, making us stronger and more complete in Him. Our triumphant spirit allows us to face these trials with joy, trusting that God is using them to prepare us for even greater things. Each difficulty becomes an opportunity to grow, to learn, and to draw closer to God, knowing that He will lead us through to victory.

This spirit of triumph also fills us with boldness as we walk in faith, sharing God's love with others. When we know that God has already won, we are not afraid to speak the truth, to stand up for what is right, and to reach out to those who are hurting. We are empowered to take risks, to step out of our comfort zones, and to pursue the mission God has placed in our hearts with courage and conviction. Ephesians 6:10-11 tells us, "Finally, my brethren, be strong in the Lord, and in the power of his might. Put on the whole armour of God, that ye may be able to stand against the wiles of the devil." This verse reminds us that we are equipped with God's strength, that He has given us everything we need to stand firm and to face any challenge. Our triumphant spirit helps us to be fearless in our mission, knowing that we are not alone and that God's power is greater than any force that might come against us.

On this journey from vision to mission, our triumphant spirit also brings joy and peace, even in the midst of trials. When we are secure in the hope of God's Kingdom, we can find joy in every situation, knowing that God is in control. We are not defeated by difficult circumstances; instead, we rise above them, trusting that God is with us and that He will bring good out of every situation. Romans 8:28 assures us, "And we know that all things work together for good to them that love God, to them who are the called according to his purpose." This promise gives us peace, knowing that God is working behind the scenes, weaving every part of our lives into a beautiful story that brings glory to Him. This triumphant spirit allows us to keep a positive outlook, to find reasons to be thankful, and to spread joy to those around us, even in the toughest times. We become beacons of hope, shining God's light and showing others that His love can overcome anything.

Our triumphant spirit on this mission also reminds us that our labor is not in vain. Sometimes, the work we do for God may feel difficult or thankless, and we may wonder if it is making a difference. But with a heart full of hope, we know that every act of kindness, every word of encouragement, and every step of faith is seen by God and is part of His Kingdom work. 1 Corinthians 15:58

encourages us, "Therefore, my beloved brethren, be ye stedfast, unmoveable, always abounding in the work of the Lord, forasmuch as ye know that your labour is not in vain in the Lord." This verse reassures us that God values our efforts, that He sees every sacrifice, and that He will bring forth fruit in His time. Our triumphant spirit allows us to keep going, even when the results are not immediately visible, trusting that God is using our work to plant seeds of faith and hope in the hearts of others.

The hope of God's Kingdom also fills us with compassion for others, as we recognize that our victory in Christ is something we are called to share. We are not meant to keep this triumphant spirit to ourselves; rather, we are called to reach out to others, to lift them up, and to show them the love and hope that God offers. When we see others struggling, our hearts are moved with compassion, and we are motivated to offer help, encouragement, and support. 2 Corinthians 1:3-4 reminds us, "Blessed be God, even the Father of our Lord Jesus Christ, the Father of mercies, and the God of all comfort; Who comforteth us in all our tribulation, that we may be able to comfort them which are in any trouble, by the comfort wherewith we ourselves are comforted of God." This verse shows us that God's comfort is not only for our benefit; it is also meant to be shared, to be a source of strength for others. Our triumphant spirit allows us to be a source of comfort and hope, helping others to see that they too can find victory in God's love.

As we continue on this trail, our triumphant spirit helps us to stay focused on the eternal goal, keeping our eyes on God's Kingdom and the joy that awaits us. The challenges of this world may weigh us down, but when we remember that our true home is with God, we find the strength to keep going. Philippians 3:13-14 encourages us, "Brethren, I count not myself to have apprehended: but this one thing I do, forgetting those things which are behind, and reaching forth unto those things which are before, I press toward the mark for the prize of the high calling of God in Christ Jesus." This verse reminds us to look forward, to keep pressing on, knowing that the reward of our faith is worth every sacrifice. Our triumphant spirit keeps us focused on God's promises, helping us to let go of past hurts and failures and to move forward with confidence in His love.

Ultimately, our triumphant spirit is rooted in the assurance that we are loved by God and that His Kingdom is unshakeable. No matter what happens, we are secure in His hands, and nothing can separate us from His love. Romans 8:38-39 declares, "For I am persuaded, that neither death, nor life, nor angels, nor principalities, nor powers, nor things present, nor things to come, Nor height, nor depth, nor any other creature, shall be able to separate us from the love of God, which is in Christ Jesus our Lord." This assurance fills us with peace, giving us the confidence to face each day with courage and hope. Our triumphant spirit reminds us that God's love is our foundation, that His Kingdom is eternal, and that we are part of a mission that cannot fail. This is the heart of our journey, our vision, and our mission—to live with a triumphant spirit, to share God's love with a world in need, and to walk in the victory that Christ has given us. This is our calling, our joy, and our hope, to shine God's light, to lift others up, and to fulfill His purpose with hearts full of joy and strength.

Chapter 17 - Tempered with Grace

The journey on the "Trail From Vision to Mission" teaches us to be tempered with grace, a quality that shapes how we serve others with love, kindness, and compassion. When we're tempered with grace, our hearts are softened and filled with understanding, allowing us to see others through God's eyes, with patience and forgiveness. Colossians 4:6 encourages us, "Let your speech be alway with grace, seasoned with salt, that ye may know how ye ought to answer every man." This verse reminds us that grace should flavor everything we say and do, adding kindness and gentleness to our words and actions. It means speaking with a tone of respect, showing empathy for others, and approaching every situation with a heart of humility and love. Being tempered with grace doesn't mean we ignore the truth or avoid hard conversations, but it does mean we handle them with a loving spirit, focused on lifting others up rather than tearing them down. We become mindful of our words, careful to speak in a way that reflects God's love and brings peace rather than conflict. Grace allows us to serve in a way that touches hearts, for people feel the love and patience behind our actions and are drawn closer to God's kindness through our example.

When our hearts are tempered with grace, we find it easier to forgive, even when others may hurt us or fall short of our expectations. We remember that we, too, are recipients of God's endless grace, that He forgives us daily and loves us despite our flaws. This understanding shapes how we treat others, filling us with a spirit of forgiveness that mirrors God's own mercy. Ephesians 4:32 encourages us, "And be ye kind one to another, tenderhearted, forgiving one another, even as God for Christ's sake hath forgiven you." This verse shows that just as God forgives us, we are called to forgive others. Grace teaches us to let go of grudges, to overlook minor offenses, and to respond to others' mistakes with patience. When we forgive freely, we create an atmosphere of love and acceptance, a safe space where people can grow and feel supported, knowing they are valued just as they are. Our ability to extend grace opens doors for healing and reconciliation, helping us to build stronger, more loving relationships with others.

Grace also helps us to be patient with people, understanding that everyone is on their own journey and that growth takes time. Each person we encounter has their own struggles, doubts, and fears, and they may not always respond the way we hope. Being tempered with grace allows us to meet people where they are, to be patient with their progress, and to encourage them gently along the way. James 1:19 reminds us, "Wherefore, my beloved brethren, let every man be swift to hear, slow to speak, slow to wrath." This wisdom teaches us to listen first, to understand before reacting, and to approach others with calm and understanding. Grace teaches us that we don't have to rush others to change or to meet our expectations; instead, we can trust that God is working in their lives at His own pace. We become patient encouragers, walking alongside others with a heart of compassion, cheering them on as they grow closer to God.

On this trail from vision to mission, being tempered with grace also helps us to be more understanding of people's struggles and needs. We begin to see that everyone has burdens they carry, challenges they face, and wounds that may not be visible. Grace opens our eyes to the deeper needs of others, helping us to see beyond surface behavior to the pain, fear, or confusion that may lie beneath. This understanding makes us more compassionate, more willing to offer a listening ear or a comforting word. Galatians 6:2 reminds us, "Bear ye one another's burdens, and so fulfil the law of Christ." When we are tempered with grace, we become willing to help carry the burdens of others, to offer support in times of trouble, and to be a friend to those who feel alone. Grace makes us sensitive to the needs around us, prompting us to reach out with love and kindness, knowing that even a small act of care can make a big difference in someone's life.

Being tempered with grace also shapes our reactions in difficult situations, helping us to respond with gentleness and self-control. There will be times when we face misunderstandings, criticism, or even unfair treatment, and it can be tempting to react with anger or defensiveness. But grace teaches us a different way, a way that reflects Christ's love and patience. Proverbs 15:1 tells us, "A soft answer turneth away wrath: but grievous words stir up anger." This verse reminds us that a gentle response can diffuse tension and bring peace, while harsh words only escalate conflict. When we are tempered with grace, we learn to choose our words carefully, to respond calmly, and to approach conflicts with a desire for peace rather than revenge. Grace gives us the strength to control our emotions, to pause before we react, and to handle challenges with a calm and steady heart. In doing so, we bring a spirit of peace into every situation, showing others that God's love is stronger than anger and that kindness can overcome even the hardest hearts.

Grace also fills us with humility, helping us to recognize our own need for God's mercy and to approach others without judgment. When we see our own weaknesses and remember how much God has forgiven us, we are less likely to look down on others or to hold ourselves above them. Instead, we become more accepting, more willing to understand rather than condemn. Romans 3:23 reminds us, "For all have sinned, and come short of the glory of God." This verse reminds us that none of us are perfect, that we all need grace, and that we are all equal in God's eyes. When we remember this truth, we approach others with a heart of humility, not as people who have it all figured out, but as fellow travelers on the same journey. Grace removes the barriers of pride and self-righteousness, allowing us to connect with others on a deeper level, to show love without judgment, and to offer support without expecting anything in return.

On this journey, being tempered with grace also helps us to be more joyful and thankful, for grace reminds us of the countless blessings God has poured into our lives. When we recognize how much we have been given, how deeply we are loved, and how often we are forgiven, our hearts overflow with gratitude. This thankfulness shapes how we interact with others, filling us with a spirit of generosity and kindness. 1 Thessalonians 5:18 encourages us, "In every thing give thanks: for this is the will of God in Christ Jesus concerning you." When we live with a thankful heart, we become more gracious toward others, more willing to overlook minor annoyances, and more eager to share the love and blessings we have received. Our joy and gratitude become contagious, lifting the spirits of those around us and creating an atmosphere of love and grace.

Being tempered with grace also means being willing to offer encouragement, to build others up, and to help them see their worth in God's eyes. Grace teaches us that each person has value, that everyone has unique gifts and strengths, and that we are all precious to God. Ephesians 4:29 tells us, "Let no corrupt communication proceed out of your mouth, but that which is good to the use of edifying, that it may minister grace unto the hearers." This verse encourages us to speak words that lift others up, that bring comfort, and that remind them of their value. When we are tempered with grace, we look for ways to encourage, to speak life into others, and to help them see the potential that God has placed within them. Our words become a source of strength and inspiration, helping others to grow in confidence and to feel loved and accepted.

Ultimately, being tempered with grace on this trail from vision to mission means living in a way that reflects God's love in everything we do. Grace is at the heart of God's character, and when we allow it to shape our lives, we become a living example of His kindness, mercy, and compassion. We become people who bring peace into conflict, who offer forgiveness instead of holding grudges, and who serve others with a joyful heart. This journey teaches us that grace is not just a gift we receive from God; it's a gift we are called to share with others. Each act of grace we show becomes a reflection of God's love, a reminder to the world that His kindness is real and available to all.

As we walk this trail, may we be tempered with grace, may we learn to see others as God sees them, and may we serve with hearts full of love and compassion. Let our actions, our words, and our attitudes be seasoned with grace, bringing hope, healing, and joy to those around us. This is our mission, our calling, and our purpose—to be vessels of God's grace, to let His love flow through us, and to make a difference in the lives of others by reflecting the beauty of His character.

Chapter 18 - Thriving in Faith

The journey on the "Trail From Vision to Mission" allows us to experience the beauty of thriving in faith, a dynamic, living faith that grows stronger with each step we take in following God's calling. Thriving in faith means that our relationship with God isn't static or stagnant; instead, it's vibrant, active, and always deepening as we walk in obedience to Him. When we commit ourselves to His mission, our faith is nurtured, stretched, and enriched in ways that we may never have expected. Hebrews 11:6 reminds us, "But without faith it is impossible to please him: for he that cometh to God must believe that he is, and that he is a rewarder of them that diligently seek him." This verse emphasizes that faith is the foundation of our relationship with God, a trust in who He is and in His promises. As we step out in faith, taking up the mission He has given us, we come to know Him in deeper and more personal ways. We learn to rely on His strength, to trust in His timing, and to see His hand at work in both the challenges and the victories we encounter. Each time we lean on Him, our faith grows a little more, and we find ourselves moving from simply believing in God to truly depending on Him in every part of our lives.

On this journey, thriving in faith means that we continue to grow, even in difficult times. Mission work often brings us face-to-face with challenges, uncertainties, and sometimes opposition, but it's in these moments that our faith has the chance to grow stronger. We learn to stand firm, to keep going even when the way is hard, because we trust that God is with us and will guide us through. James 1:3-4 encourages us, "Knowing this, that the trying of your faith worketh patience. But let patience have her perfect work, that ye may be perfect and entire, wanting nothing." This passage reminds us that trials are not meant to defeat us but to build us up, to develop patience, and to help us grow into maturity. As we press on in our mission, our faith matures, becoming more resilient and more deeply rooted in God's love and promises. Each trial we overcome becomes a testimony of God's faithfulness, a reminder that He is with us, and that He uses every challenge to shape us into people who reflect His strength and grace.

Thriving in faith also means experiencing joy and peace, even in the midst of uncertainty. Faith is not just a feeling; it's a confidence in God that allows us to face life's ups and downs with a steady heart. When we are rooted in faith, we are not easily shaken, because we know that God is in control. Philippians 4:6-7 tells us, "Be careful for nothing; but in every thing by prayer and supplication with thanksgiving let your requests be made known unto God. And the peace of God, which passeth all understanding, shall keep your hearts and minds through Christ Jesus." This verse reminds us that faith brings peace, a peace that goes beyond our understanding and keeps us steady in all circumstances. As we walk in faith, trusting God with our worries and challenges, we find a joy that is not dependent on circumstances but rooted in His presence. This joy and peace are signs of a thriving faith, a faith that isn't discouraged by setbacks but is constantly renewed by the hope we have in God.

Our mission work also nurtures a thriving faith by bringing us closer to God, deepening our relationship with Him as we spend time in prayer, seek His guidance, and rely on His wisdom. Each time we pray, each time we seek His will, we draw closer to Him, and our understanding of His love grows. Jeremiah 29:13 promises, "And ye shall seek me, and find me, when ye shall search for me with all your heart." This verse reminds us that God reveals Himself to those who seek Him sincerely, and as we pursue His mission, we experience His presence in new and powerful ways. Our relationship with God becomes more personal, more intimate, as we come to know Him not just as a distant figure, but as a loving Father who is involved in every detail of our lives. Through mission work, we learn to listen to His voice, to follow His lead, and to trust His plan, growing closer to Him with each step we take.

Thriving in faith also fills us with courage, giving us the boldness to step out of our comfort zones and to do things we might not have thought possible. Mission work often calls us to unfamiliar places or asks us to reach out to people we don't know, but with faith, we find the courage to go forward, knowing that God is with us. Joshua 1:9 reminds us, "Have not I commanded thee? Be strong and of a good courage; be not afraid, neither be thou dismayed: for the Lord thy God is with thee whithersoever thou goest." This verse gives us confidence, reminding us that we are not alone, that God is with us, and that He empowers us to do His work. As we take steps of faith, whether big or small, our confidence grows, and we become more willing to follow where God leads, trusting that He will equip us and guide us in every situation.

On this trail, thriving in faith also means developing a heart of compassion for others, as we see the world through God's eyes. Mission work opens our hearts, helping us to see the needs, struggles, and hopes of those around us, and this deepens our desire to share God's love. Matthew 9:36 shows us Jesus' compassion, saying, "But when he saw the multitudes, he was moved with compassion on them, because they fainted, and were scattered abroad, as sheep having no shepherd." This verse reminds us that faith is not just about our relationship with God but also about loving others as He does. Thriving in faith means that our hearts are softened, that we feel a genuine compassion for others, and that we are motivated to serve, to help, and to share the hope we have found in Christ. Our faith becomes a living testimony, a reflection of God's love that reaches out to those in need and shows them that they are valued and loved by Him.

This thriving faith also keeps us focused on the eternal, helping us to remember that our mission work has a purpose that goes beyond this life. When we are rooted in faith, we live with a sense of purpose, knowing that our actions, our words, and our efforts are part of God's Kingdom work. Colossians 3:2 encourages us, "Set your affection on things above, not on things on the earth." This verse reminds us to keep our eyes on God's Kingdom, to live for things that have eternal value, and to let our faith guide us toward a life of meaning and purpose. Thriving in faith means we are not distracted by temporary things; instead, we are focused on serving God, sharing His love, and making a difference that lasts beyond this life.

A thriving faith on this trail also strengthens our hope, giving us confidence in God's promises and in the future He has prepared for us. Faith fills us with hope, a hope that looks forward with joy, knowing that God's promises are true and that He is faithful. Romans 15:13 reminds us, "Now the God of hope fill you with all joy and peace in believing, that ye may abound in hope, through the power of the Holy Ghost." This verse shows us that faith and hope go hand in hand, that our trust in God leads to a life filled with joy and anticipation. As we walk this trail, we hold onto God's promises, knowing that He is preparing something wonderful for us, both in this life and in the life to come. Our hope becomes a source of strength, a reminder that no matter what we face, God is with us, and His love will carry us through.

Ultimately, thriving in faith means living a life that reflects God's love, a life that shows the world that His love is real, powerful, and life-changing. Our mission work becomes a way to live out our faith, to share the hope, joy, and love that God has given us, and to be a light in a world that needs His truth. Matthew 5:16 encourages us, "Let your light so shine before men, that they may see your good works, and glorify your Father which is in heaven." This verse reminds us that our faith is not just for ourselves; it is meant to be shared, to be a beacon of hope, and to draw others closer to God. Thriving in faith means that our lives become a testimony, a way to point others to God and to show them that His love is real and available to them.

As we continue on this trail, may we grow stronger in faith, may we trust God more deeply, and may we experience the joy and peace that come from knowing Him. Let our faith be a living, thriving force that shapes everything we do, that guides us in our mission, and that brings us closer to God each day. This is our calling, our purpose, and our joy—to thrive in faith, to walk in God's love, and to fulfill the mission He has placed in our hearts with a spirit of courage, compassion, and unwavering trust in His promises. This journey from vision to mission is a path of growth, a trail that leads us closer to God, and a life filled with hope, joy, and a faith that continues to thrive.

Chapter 19 - Tactical Wisdom

The journey on the "Trail From Vision to Mission" shows us the importance of tactical wisdom, a kind of guidance and insight that comes only from God and helps us reach others effectively. This wisdom is more than just knowledge; it's an understanding given by God that enables us to speak and act in ways that truly touch hearts and bring people closer to Him. When we seek to share God's love, we want to do it in the best way possible, in a way that really resonates with others and meets them where they are. In James 1:5, we are told, "If any of you lack wisdom, let him ask of God, that giveth to all men liberally, and upbraideth not; and it shall be given him." This verse reminds us that God is ready to pour out His wisdom upon us if we simply ask. He is generous with His guidance, eager to help us make wise choices that honor Him and serve His purpose. Tactical wisdom involves knowing when to speak, when to listen, and when to act. It's about being sensitive to the needs of those around us and asking God to guide our steps so that we can make the greatest impact for His Kingdom. Each person we encounter has their own story, struggles, and hopes, and without God's wisdom, it can be hard to know the right words to say or the best way to help. But when we are open to His guidance, He shows us exactly how to approach each situation with love, patience, and understanding.

Tactical wisdom also helps us to see beyond appearances, to look deeper into people's hearts, and to understand their true needs. Sometimes, people may put on a brave face or hide their struggles, but God's wisdom allows us to discern what lies beneath the surface. Proverbs 3:5-6 encourages us, "Trust in the Lord with all thine heart; and lean not unto thine own understanding. In all thy ways acknowledge him, and he shall direct thy paths." This wisdom teaches us to rely on God's understanding rather than our own, to let Him direct our actions and words so that we can reach others in meaningful ways. By leaning on God's wisdom, we avoid the temptation to judge or make assumptions, and instead, we approach each person with a heart of compassion and a desire to understand. Tactical wisdom helps us see beyond what we think we know and allows us to connect with people in a way that feels genuine, caring, and thoughtful. It teaches us to ask questions, to listen well, and to offer support in ways that are truly helpful rather than just superficial.

On this trail from vision to mission, tactical wisdom also guides us in how we share the message of God's love and truth. Different people respond to different approaches, and God's wisdom helps us to communicate in ways that are clear, gentle, and relevant to each person's situation. Colossians 4:6 advises, "Let your speech be alway with grace, seasoned with salt, that ye may know how ye ought to answer every man." This verse reminds us that our words should be filled with kindness and respect, seasoned with truth and love, so that they uplift and encourage others. Tactical wisdom helps us choose words that bring comfort and hope rather than words that might discourage or push someone away. Sometimes, a gentle approach is needed, while other times, a direct conversation is more effective. With God's guidance, we can discern the right tone and message, making it easier for others to open their hearts to His love.

Tactical wisdom also helps us recognize opportunities, those moments when someone may be open to hearing about God or when a small act of kindness could make a big difference. These opportunities are often subtle, like a quiet comment or a look of sadness, but God's wisdom enables us to notice them and respond. Ecclesiastes 3:1 tells us, "To every thing there is a season, and a time to every purpose under the heaven." This verse reminds us that God has a timing for everything, and tactical wisdom helps us to act at the right time. When we are in tune with His guidance, we can seize these moments, planting seeds of faith and hope in the lives of those we meet. God's wisdom helps us to be present, to be aware of those around us, and to recognize the ways we can be a light, even in the smallest gestures.

This journey also teaches us that tactical wisdom includes humility. Sometimes, we may feel like we know the right answers or have the perfect plan, but true wisdom means being open to God's leading and willing to adjust our plans when He shows us a better way. Proverbs 16:9 says, "A man's heart deviseth his way: but the Lord directeth his steps." Tactical wisdom means trusting that God's way is best, even when it differs from our own understanding. It means being willing to listen to others, to learn, and to admit when we don't have all the answers. Humility allows us to be flexible, to let go of our own ideas, and to follow God's guidance with an open heart. This humility makes it easier for us to connect with others, as they see that we are not trying to control or force our beliefs but are genuinely seeking to serve and help in the way God leads.

Being tempered with tactical wisdom also helps us to maintain patience, especially when we don't see immediate results. Sometimes, reaching others takes time, and it's easy to become discouraged if things don't happen as quickly as we hope. But wisdom teaches us that God's timing is perfect, and we can trust that He is working even when we can't see it. Isaiah 55:8-9 reminds us, "For my thoughts are not your thoughts, neither are your ways my ways, saith the Lord. For as the heavens are higher than the earth, so are my ways higher than your ways, and my thoughts than your thoughts." This verse encourages us to trust in God's plan, to be patient, and to keep moving forward even when progress seems slow. Tactical wisdom gives us the strength to persevere, knowing that each small step, each kind word, and each prayer is part of God's bigger plan.

Tactical wisdom also fills us with compassion, helping us to serve others with empathy and understanding. When we seek God's wisdom, He softens our hearts, helping us to approach others with a desire to understand rather than judge. We begin to see people through His eyes, understanding that everyone has struggles, fears, and hopes. James 3:17 describes this kind of wisdom, saying, "But the wisdom that is from above is first pure, then peaceable, gentle, and easy to be intreated, full of mercy and good fruits, without partiality, and without hypocrisy." This verse shows us that God's wisdom is gentle and full of mercy, a wisdom that brings peace and builds bridges. When our hearts are filled with this wisdom, we can reach others in a way that feels welcoming and genuine, showing them that they are valued and loved by God.

On this journey, tactical wisdom also guides us in setting boundaries, helping us to serve effectively without becoming overwhelmed. Sometimes, the needs around us can feel endless, and it's easy to become exhausted if we try to do everything on our own. But God's wisdom teaches us to know our limits, to rely on His strength, and to trust Him to take care of the things we can't. Matthew 11:28-30 encourages us, "Come unto me, all ye that labour and are heavy laden, and I will give you rest. Take my yoke upon you, and learn of me; for I am meek and lowly in heart: and ye shall find rest unto your souls. For my yoke is easy, and my burden is light." This promise reminds us that we don't have to carry every burden alone, that God is with us, guiding us and giving us rest. Tactical wisdom allows us to serve without burning out, to trust God to handle what we can't, and to find joy in knowing that He is in control.

Ultimately, tactical wisdom on this trail from vision to mission is about seeking God's guidance in every decision, trusting Him to show us the best way to reach others. It's about letting Him shape our hearts, fill us with compassion, and guide our words and actions so that they reflect His love. Each time we ask for His wisdom, we draw closer to Him, learning to rely on His strength and to trust in His perfect plan. This wisdom not only helps us to be more effective in our mission but also deepens our relationship with God, as we come to know Him as our guide, our source of strength, and our closest friend.

As we continue on this journey, may we be filled with God's wisdom, may we trust in His guidance, and may we reach others with a heart full of love and compassion. This is our mission, our calling, and our purpose—to walk in God's wisdom, to share His love effectively, and to fulfill the vision He has given us with humility, patience, and a heart that is open to His leading.

Chapter 20 - Taking Heart

The journey on the "Trail From Vision to Mission" teaches us to take heart, to stand strong and be courageous, even when we know challenges will come. Taking heart means holding onto courage, leaning on God's strength, and finding peace in His promises, no matter what we face. Jesus tells us in John 16:33, "These things I have spoken unto you, that in me ye might have peace. In the world ye shall have tribulation: but be of good cheer; I have overcome the world." This verse reminds us that while difficulties are part of life, we don't have to fear them, because Jesus has already conquered the world. Taking heart is about finding hope and courage, knowing that God is with us, guiding us, and that we can trust in His unfailing love and power. As we move from vision to mission, stepping into the calling God has placed on our lives, we will inevitably encounter obstacles. These may come in the form of doubts, opposition, or moments of feeling overwhelmed. Yet, when we take heart, we choose to focus not on the size of the challenge, but on the greatness of our God. We remember that He is faithful, that He goes before us, and that His promises are our solid ground. Each step forward becomes an act of trust, a declaration that we believe in His power and His love for us.

Taking heart also involves holding onto hope, even when things don't go as planned. Sometimes, we may face setbacks, delays, or unexpected difficulties on our mission, but taking heart means we don't give up. We press on, knowing that God is working behind the scenes, shaping us, and guiding our path. Romans 8:28 reminds us, "And we know that all things work together for good to them that love God, to them who are the called according to his purpose." This promise assures us that God is always at work, weaving even the hard moments into a bigger plan that leads to good. Taking heart means clinging to this hope, trusting that God's purpose will prevail, and that every struggle is part of the journey He is using to strengthen our faith. Each difficulty becomes an opportunity to grow closer to Him, to learn to rely on His strength, and to see His faithfulness in new ways. Taking heart means choosing joy even in trials, finding comfort in the knowledge that we are never alone, and that God's grace is enough to carry us through anything we face.

On this trail, taking heart also means standing firm in our faith, even when the world around us feels uncertain. There may be times when our mission seems difficult, when doubts creep in, or when we feel like we're not making a difference. But taking heart reminds us to hold onto what we know to be true—that God has called us, that He is faithful, and that His Word is unchanging. Hebrews 10:23 encourages us, "Let us hold fast the profession of our faith without wavering; (for he is faithful that promised)." This verse calls us to stand strong, to hold firmly to our faith, because God will not let us down. Taking heart means that we don't let circumstances shake our trust in God. Instead, we root ourselves in His promises, finding courage in the truth that He is always with us, and that His love will never fail. We remind ourselves of the times He has been faithful in the past, using these memories as stones of remembrance that build our confidence in Him.

Taking heart also involves being prepared to face opposition with a spirit of peace and love. As we follow God's mission, there may be people who don't understand, who criticize, or who try to discourage us. But taking heart means we don't let these voices deter us. Instead, we remember that our strength comes from God, not from the approval or understanding of others. Galatians 1:10 reminds us, "For do I now persuade men, or God? or do I seek to please men? for if I yet pleased men, I should not be the servant of Christ." This verse encourages us to focus on God's approval, knowing that His opinion is what matters most. Taking heart means being willing to stand up for what we believe in, to keep going even when others don't agree, and to do it all with a heart of love and respect. We don't respond with anger or frustration; instead, we remain calm, kind, and focused on the mission God has given us, knowing that He sees our hearts and honors our faithfulness.

Taking heart on this journey also means relying on God's strength when we feel weak or discouraged. There will be times when we feel tired, when the road feels long, and when we wonder if we have what it takes. But taking heart reminds us that we don't have to rely on our own strength. 2 Corinthians 12:9 teaches us, "And he said unto me, My grace is sufficient for thee: for my strength is made perfect in weakness." This verse assures us that God's grace is more than enough, and that His power shines through in our moments of weakness. Taking heart means surrendering our struggles to God, allowing His strength to carry us when we can't carry ourselves. We learn to lean on Him, to trust that He will give us what we need each day, and to find peace in the knowledge that His power is at work within us. Taking heart isn't about pretending to be strong; it's about acknowledging our need for God and finding our strength in Him alone.

This journey also shows us that taking heart involves looking to the future with hope and expectation, confident that God's promises will come to pass. We are not just walking through this life aimlessly; we are headed toward a glorious future with God, a Kingdom that He has prepared for those who love Him. Jeremiah 29:11 reminds us, "For I know the thoughts that I think toward you, saith the Lord, thoughts of peace, and not of evil, to give you an expected end." This verse gives us hope, assuring us that God has good plans for us and that His purpose will be fulfilled. Taking heart means we live with our eyes on the eternal, knowing that the struggles of this life are temporary and that the joy of being with God forever is worth every sacrifice. We find courage in this hope, allowing it to sustain us in hard times, and it becomes the light that guides us forward, reminding us that our mission has eternal significance.

Ultimately, taking heart on the trail from vision to mission is about embracing God's promises, finding courage in His love, and walking each day with a spirit of hope. It's a journey that teaches us resilience, helping us to keep going when the way is hard, to trust when we don't understand, and to love even when it's challenging. Taking heart means we don't let fear, doubt, or discouragement hold us back; instead, we let God's promises be our foundation, our source of strength, and our reason to keep pressing on. With each step we take, we draw closer to Him, our faith grows stronger, and our hearts become more attuned to His love. This is our mission, our calling, and our joy—to take heart, to stand firm in God's promises, and to live with a hope that cannot be shaken. This journey from vision to mission is not always easy, but with God by our side, we can face every challenge, knowing that He has already overcome the world. This is our strength, our courage, and our peace: that no matter what lies ahead, we can take heart, for God is with us, guiding us and leading us every step of the way.

Chapter 21 - Truth as Foundation

The journey on the "Trail From Vision to Mission" is built upon the unwavering foundation of truth, a truth that comes from God alone and never changes, no matter the circumstances. This truth is what gives us confidence, purpose, and direction in our mission, grounding us in something real and eternal. Jesus prayed in John 17:17, "Sanctify them through thy truth: thy word is truth." This verse reminds us that God's Word is the ultimate truth, a solid rock on which we can stand, even when the world around us feels uncertain or confusing. In a world where ideas, values, and opinions shift constantly, the truth of God's Word remains the same, providing us with a reliable guide for how to live, love, and serve. This truth tells us who God is—faithful, loving, and just—and who we are in His eyes, beloved and called with purpose. When we stand on this foundation, we are not easily swayed by doubts, fears, or the pressures of society. We know who we serve, why we are here, and what God has called us to do. His truth becomes the compass that directs our path, helping us to make wise choices, to walk in love, and to fulfill our mission with integrity and faith.

The truth of God's Word also equips us to stand strong against the lies and challenges we may face. As we walk this mission, there will be times when we encounter opposition, doubt, or even deception. But God's truth is our shield, protecting us from anything that would try to shake our faith or lead us astray. Ephesians 6:14 encourages us to "Stand therefore, having your loins girt about with truth." This verse calls us to "put on" truth, to hold it close to our hearts so that it becomes part of who we are. When we are grounded in God's truth, we are able to discern right from wrong, to recognize when something doesn't align with His Word, and to stay rooted in His promises. This foundation gives us courage, allowing us to face difficult situations with clarity and conviction, knowing that God's Word is the final authority in all things. When the storms of life come, when doubts arise, or when others question our mission, we can stand firm, not because of our own strength, but because we are anchored in the unchanging truth of God.

Truth as our foundation also reminds us of the importance of honesty and integrity in our mission. God's truth calls us to live with honesty, to let our actions and words reflect the sincerity of our faith. Proverbs 12:22 tells us, "Lying lips are abomination to the Lord: but they that deal truly are his delight." This verse encourages us to be truthful in all that we do, to be people who can be trusted, and to let our lives be a reflection of God's own honesty and goodness. When we live with integrity, we build trust with those around us, showing them that our faith is real and that our love is genuine. In a world that often values convenience over honesty, standing on God's truth sets us apart, making our lives a testimony of His love and faithfulness. Each time we choose to be honest, even when it's difficult, we are honoring God and showing others that His truth is worth living out.

Standing on God's truth also gives us purpose, helping us to see that our mission is not just about ourselves but about something much greater. God's truth reveals His heart for humanity, His desire to reach the lost, and His call for us to be part of His Kingdom work. John 8:32 reminds us, "And ye shall know the truth, and the truth shall make you free." This freedom is not just for us; it is something we are called to share with others. Knowing the truth of God's love and salvation motivates us to reach out, to spread the good news, and to help others find the freedom we have experienced. We realize that our mission has eternal significance, that every act of kindness, every word of hope, and every moment spent serving others is part of God's plan to draw people closer to Him. This truth fills our hearts with purpose, helping us to stay focused and dedicated to the work God has called us to do.

The truth of God's Word also shapes how we see others, filling us with compassion and a desire to love as Jesus loved. When we know the truth of God's love for each person, it changes the way we treat them, showing us that every individual is valuable and cherished by God. Galatians 5:14 reminds us, "For all the law is fulfilled in one word, even in this; Thou shalt love thy neighbour as thyself." Standing on God's truth means that we are committed to loving others, to showing kindness, and to serving with humility. This foundation of truth helps us to be patient, to forgive, and to be understanding, even when others may be difficult to love. We don't serve for recognition or reward; we serve because God's truth has transformed our hearts and filled us with a desire to reflect His love to the world.

Truth as our foundation also helps us to endure, to keep going even when the journey is hard. There will be times when our mission feels challenging, when we face obstacles or feel weary. But the truth of God's promises gives us the strength to persevere. Philippians 4:13 encourages us, "I can do all things through Christ which strengtheneth me." This promise reminds us that we are not alone, that God is with us, and that His strength will carry us through. When we stand on His truth, we know that His grace is sufficient, that His love is constant, and that He will never leave us nor forsake us. This foundation gives us the courage to press on, to keep serving, and to trust that God will provide everything we need to fulfill His mission.

This foundation of truth also fills us with hope, a hope that is not based on circumstances but on the faithfulness of God. Hebrews 6:19 describes this hope as "an anchor of the soul, both sure and stedfast." When we build our lives on God's truth, we are anchored in His promises, and nothing can shake us. We know that God's Kingdom is unshakable, that His love is eternal, and that His purpose for us is good. This hope gives us joy, even in trials, and it becomes a light that we can share with others. As we serve and reach out, this hope shines through, showing others that God's truth is a source of peace and joy, no matter what life may bring.

Ultimately, truth as our foundation means living a life that is centered on God, allowing His Word to guide us, shape us, and inspire us. Each step we take on this trail from vision to mission is anchored in the truth of who God is and what He has promised. This journey may not always be easy, but with God's truth as our foundation, we can move forward with confidence, knowing that we are part of something eternal. This is our mission, our purpose, and our joy—to live in God's truth, to share His love, and to build our lives on the solid rock of His Word. This journey from vision to mission is a path of faith, hope, and love, a trail that leads us closer to God and allows us to be part of His incredible plan for the world. Standing on His truth, we are unshakable, filled with purpose, and ready to fulfill the mission He has given us.

Chapter 22 - Turning from Distractions

The journey on the "Trail From Vision to Mission" requires us to turn from distractions and stay focused on God's purpose, keeping our eyes fixed on the path He has set before us. In today's world, distractions are everywhere, constantly pulling our attention away from what really matters. From the busyness of daily life to the endless flood of information, entertainment, and social pressures, it's easy to lose sight of our mission. Yet, Colossians 3:2 urges us, "Set your affection on things above, not on things on the earth." This verse reminds us that our hearts and minds should be focused on heavenly things, on God's purpose for our lives, rather than being consumed by the temporary things of this world. Staying focused means we actively choose to turn away from distractions that can pull us off course, and instead, we commit to following God's vision with clarity and purpose. Turning from distractions isn't just about saying "no" to certain things; it's about saying "yes" to the life God has called us to, a life filled with meaning, love, and a mission that impacts the world around us. When we focus on His purpose, our days take on a new depth, filled with moments where we can serve, grow, and bring hope to others. Each time we turn from distractions, we remind ourselves that God's calling is worth our full attention, and we find joy in knowing that we are walking the path He has designed just for us.

Turning from distractions requires a heart of discipline and commitment, where we choose to let go of anything that competes for our attention and drains our energy from what God has called us to do. There are many things that may be good or enjoyable, but if they don't align with our mission or pull us away from spending time with God, they can become hindrances. Hebrews 12:1 encourages us to "lay aside every weight, and the sin which doth so easily beset us, and let us run with patience the race that is set before us." This verse teaches us that if we want to follow God's purpose wholeheartedly, we must be willing to remove anything that holds us back, so that we can run our race with strength and focus. Distractions are like weights, slowing us down, making it harder to see the path ahead clearly. But as we turn from them, as we strip away those things that do not serve our purpose, we find a newfound freedom and energy to pursue God's mission with all our heart.

Staying focused also means learning to be content with the simplicity of God's path, rather than being drawn to the constant lure of "more" that the world offers. We live in a world that tells us we need more—more possessions, more achievements, more approval from others. But God calls us to a life that values quality over quantity, a life that seeks depth and purpose rather than endless pursuits. 1 Timothy 6:6 reminds us, "But godliness with contentment is great gain." When we focus on God's purpose, we begin to find contentment in His provision, knowing that what He gives us is enough. We stop comparing ourselves to others, stop chasing after things that do not satisfy, and instead, we find joy in knowing we are doing what He has asked of us. Each time we turn from the distractions of worldly success or approval, we draw closer to a place of peace, knowing that our worth is not found in what we have, but in who we are in Christ.

Turning from distractions also means being intentional with our time, choosing to prioritize the things that bring us closer to God and help us grow in our mission. Time is a precious gift, and once it's gone, we can't get it back. When we spend too much time on things that don't matter—whether it's scrolling through social media, worrying about what others think, or getting caught up in endless activities—we lose valuable moments that could have been used to deepen our relationship with God or to serve others. Psalm 90:12 says, "So teach us to number our days, that we may apply our hearts unto wisdom." This verse encourages us to use our time wisely, to recognize that each day is an opportunity to live with purpose, to love, to learn, and to serve. When we turn from distractions and focus on what truly matters, we make room for God to work in our lives in powerful ways, opening doors for growth, for relationships, and for impacting others with His love.

On this trail, turning from distractions also strengthens our relationship with God, as we make time to seek Him in prayer, in reading His Word, and in worship. Distractions can keep us from spending quality time with God, filling our minds with noise and leaving little room for His voice. But when we set aside distractions and turn our focus to Him, we begin to hear Him more clearly, to understand His will more fully, and to feel His presence more deeply. James 4:8 tells us, "Draw nigh to God, and he will draw nigh to you." This verse promises that when we make the effort to seek God, to draw close to Him, He will come close to us. Turning from distractions is an act of drawing near, a way of saying, "God, You are my priority." As we do this, our relationship with Him grows stronger, our faith deepens, and our hearts become more aligned with His purpose. We find that God's presence fills the places where distractions once held sway, bringing us peace, joy, and a sense of direction that cannot be found anywhere else.

Focusing on God's mission also means being willing to endure and push through when distractions come in the form of challenges or discouragement. There will be times when difficulties arise, when we feel tired or discouraged, and it's tempting to give up or to seek comfort in temporary distractions. But turning from distractions means choosing to persevere, to keep moving forward, even when the way is hard. 2 Corinthians 4:17-18 encourages us, "For our light affliction, which is but for a moment, worketh for us a far more exceeding and eternal weight of glory; While we look not at the things which are seen, but at the things which are not seen." This passage reminds us that the struggles we face are temporary, that they have a purpose, and that we are to keep our focus on the eternal. Turning from distractions means we don't let hard times pull us off course, but instead, we stay committed to God's purpose, trusting that He will carry us through and that our perseverance will lead to lasting growth and impact.

Turning from distractions also involves guarding our minds and hearts, being mindful of what we allow to influence us. In a world filled with messages that often contradict God's truth, it's essential to be vigilant, choosing to focus on things that uplift and encourage our faith. Philippians 4:8 advises us, "Finally, brethren, whatsoever things are true, whatsoever things are honest, whatsoever things are just, whatsoever things are pure, whatsoever things are lovely, whatsoever things are of good report; if there be any virtue, and if there be any praise, think on these things." This verse shows us that our thoughts matter and that we are to fill our minds with things that reflect God's goodness. By turning from distractions and focusing on what is true, we protect our hearts from negativity, fear, and doubt, allowing God's peace to fill our lives and keep us steady on our mission.

Ultimately, turning from distractions on this trail from vision to mission is about living with intentionality, choosing each day to align our lives with God's purpose. It's about waking up with a sense of direction, knowing that our lives are not random, but are part of a greater plan. Each time we turn from distractions, we are saying "yes" to the life God has designed for us, a life filled with meaning, joy, and a mission that matters. Our focus becomes clearer, our steps more deliberate, and our hearts more attuned to His voice. This journey requires discipline, but the rewards are endless—a deeper relationship with God, a sense of fulfillment, and the joy of knowing that we are making a difference for His Kingdom.

As we continue on this trail, may we have the strength and courage to turn from distractions, to keep our eyes fixed on God's purpose, and to live each day with a heart fully committed to His mission. This is our calling, our purpose, and our joy—to walk in God's vision, to serve with focus, and to fulfill the mission He has placed in our hearts. With each step, we draw closer to Him, become more like Christ, and bring His light to a world in need. This is the path from vision to mission, a journey that transforms us, that fills us with purpose, and that leads us to a life that is truly centered on God's unchanging love and truth.

Chapter 23 - Teaching by Example

The journey on the "Trail From Vision to Mission" calls us to teach by example, living in a way that shows God's love to everyone around us. Our actions, words, and attitudes become the best testimony of our faith, inspiring others to see and understand what it means to follow Christ. In 1 Timothy 4:12, Paul encourages young Timothy by saying, "Let no man despise thy youth; but be thou an example of the believers, in word, in conversation, in charity, in spirit, in faith, in purity." This verse reminds us that no matter our age, background, or situation, we can set a powerful example for others by living out our faith sincerely and openly. People are watching how we act, how we respond to challenges, and how we treat others. When we live as examples of God's love, we are teaching without even saying a word, showing the world that following Jesus is not just about words or beliefs—it's a way of life, filled with kindness, patience, and compassion. Teaching by example is about letting God's love transform every part of who we are, so that our lives become a reflection of His grace and truth.

Being a living example means embodying the qualities of Jesus in all that we do. In every interaction, whether with family, friends, or strangers, we strive to show love, patience, and respect, even when it's difficult. Jesus taught by example, not only with His words but with His actions. He healed the sick, fed the hungry, forgave those who wronged Him, and showed compassion to the outcasts. Following His example, we are called to serve others selflessly, to go out of our way to help those in need, and to show grace to those who may not always deserve it. Matthew 5:16 encourages us, "Let your light so shine before men, that they may see your good works, and glorify your Father which is in heaven." This verse reminds us that our actions have the power to point others to God. Each time we choose kindness over anger, forgiveness over bitterness, and patience over frustration, we are teaching others about God's love through our example. We don't have to be perfect, but we do need to be genuine, allowing God to work through us so that His love shines brightly in everything we do.

Living as an example also requires us to be consistent, showing the same love and faithfulness in all areas of our lives. It's easy to act kindly when things are going well, but teaching by example means staying true to our values even when life is hard. People notice our behavior during tough times—when we're under pressure, facing disappointments, or dealing with challenges. If we remain steadfast in our faith, trusting God and showing grace in those moments, we show others that our faith is real and grounded in something unshakeable. James 1:22 reminds us, "But be ye doers of the word, and not hearers only, deceiving your own selves." This verse challenges us to live out our beliefs, to put God's teachings into action rather than just talking about them. When our actions align with our words, we become credible examples, and others are more likely to trust and respect the message we share. Consistency in our walk with God is key to teaching by example, because it shows that our faith is not just a part of our lives but the foundation of everything we do.

On this trail from vision to mission, teaching by example also involves humility, acknowledging that we are still learning and growing in our own walk with God. We don't have all the answers, and we make mistakes just like everyone else. But when we are humble and open about our journey, people can see that being a follower of Christ isn't about being perfect—it's about relying on God's grace and continually seeking to become more like Him. Proverbs 3:34 tells us, "Surely he scorneth the scorners: but he giveth grace unto the lowly." This verse reminds us that God values humility and blesses those who recognize their need for Him. When we approach others with humility, we teach them that it's okay to have weaknesses and struggles, that God's love is there for us no matter what, and that our worth is not based on our accomplishments but on His love for us. Our humility allows us to connect with others on a deeper level, showing them that we are all in need of God's mercy and that His love is big enough for everyone.

Teaching by example also means being willing to forgive and to ask for forgiveness. As followers of Christ, we know that forgiveness is a central part of our faith, and showing forgiveness to others is one of the most powerful ways to demonstrate God's love. When we let go of grudges, choose to forgive those who hurt us, and seek reconciliation, we reflect the grace that God has shown us. Ephesians 4:32 encourages us, "And be ye kind one to another, tenderhearted, forgiving one another, even as God for Christ's sake hath forgiven you." This verse reminds us that our ability to forgive others flows from the forgiveness we have received from God. When we forgive, we are teaching others that God's love is unconditional, that it is possible to let go of past hurts, and that healing is available to all who seek it. Forgiveness is not always easy, but it is one of the most beautiful ways to show others the heart of God, inviting them to experience His love and mercy in their own lives.

Teaching by example also requires us to be joyful, to find hope and peace in God, even in the midst of trials. The way we handle challenges can inspire others to find strength in God. When people see that we can face difficulties with a positive spirit, trusting that God is in control, they may be encouraged to seek Him in their own lives. Romans 15:13 encourages us, "Now the God of hope fill you with all joy and peace in believing, that ye may abound in hope, through the power of the Holy Ghost." This verse reminds us that our joy and peace come from God, and they are gifts we can share with others. By showing joy in our journey, even when it's tough, we are teaching others that faith in God brings a peace that the world cannot give. Our lives become a testament to His faithfulness, showing others that no matter what we face, God's love is always with us.

Being a living example of God's love also means being available and attentive to the needs of others, showing kindness in big and small ways. Whether it's offering a listening ear, lending a helping hand, or simply being present for someone who needs comfort, our actions speak volumes. Galatians 6:2 instructs us, "Bear ye one another's burdens, and so fulfil the law of Christ." This verse calls us to support each other, to carry each other's burdens, and to show that we genuinely care. When we make time for others, we are teaching by example that love is active, that it goes beyond words and requires us to invest in the lives of those around us. Our willingness to be there for others reflects God's love, showing them that they are valued and that they are not alone.

Ultimately, teaching by example on this trail from vision to mission is about living in a way that mirrors the character of Christ, allowing His love to shine through every part of our lives. We may never know the full impact of our actions, but God uses even the smallest acts of kindness, patience, and compassion to touch hearts and draw people to Him. Our lives become a living testimony, a way for others to see God's love in action, and this is often more powerful than any words we could say. As we continue on this journey, may we be mindful of the example we set, seeking to live in a way that honors God and reflects His love to the world. This is our mission, our purpose, and our joy—to teach by example, to live with integrity, and to show others the beauty of a life lived for God. This journey from vision to mission is a calling that transforms us, strengthens our faith, and allows us to be a light in a world that needs to see God's love in action.

Chapter 24 - Total Dependence on God

The journey on the "Trail From Vision to Mission" is all about learning total dependence on God, recognizing that we cannot accomplish anything on our own and need His strength for every single step. When God places a vision in our hearts, a calling to serve others and bring His love to the world, it becomes clear that the task is far greater than we could ever handle by ourselves. We are reminded of this truth in Psalm 62:8, which says, "Trust in him at all times; ye people, pour out your heart before him: God is a refuge for us. Selah." This verse encourages us to lean on God fully, to pour out our hearts to Him in times of need, and to trust Him as our safe place and source of strength. Depending on God means we admit our own limitations and understand that He alone is the One who can carry us through. It's a humbling experience because it requires us to let go of our pride, our desire for control, and our need to handle everything ourselves. Instead, we surrender, trusting that God knows best, that His timing is perfect, and that His power is enough to handle whatever comes our way. Each step we take on this mission reminds us of our need for God, not just once in a while but every single day, in every single moment.

Total dependence on God is about trusting Him even when we cannot see the whole path ahead. Often, God's vision for us may be unclear or feel uncertain, and it takes faith to move forward without knowing exactly how everything will turn out. Proverbs 3:5-6 encourages us, "Trust in the Lord with all thine heart; and lean not unto thine own understanding. In all thy ways acknowledge him, and he shall direct thy paths." This means we have to trust God more than our own understanding, believing that He will guide us as we acknowledge Him in everything we do. This dependence gives us peace, even when we face unknowns, because we know that God is in control and will provide the direction we need, right when we need it. It's like stepping onto a bridge that only appears as we take each step forward. Depending on God in this way helps us to grow in faith, to let go of our worries, and to believe that He will make a way even when there seems to be no way. Each step on this journey is an exercise in trust, a chance to deepen our reliance on God, and an opportunity to experience His faithfulness in a personal and powerful way.

Depending on God also means turning to Him for strength when we feel weak, tired, or discouraged. There will be times on this trail when we feel like giving up, when the weight of the mission seems too heavy, or when we feel inadequate. But it's in these moments of weakness that God's strength becomes real to us. 2 Corinthians 12:9 says, "And he said unto me, My grace is sufficient for thee: for my strength is made perfect in weakness." This verse reminds us that God's grace is all we need and that His strength is made perfect in our weakness. When we lean on God, He fills us with the strength to keep going, even when we feel like we have nothing left to give. This dependence on God's strength reminds us that we don't have to carry the burden alone; He is always with us, ready to lift us up and help us through. By depending on Him, we find a source of power that goes beyond our own abilities, allowing us to overcome challenges, endure hardships, and accomplish things we never thought possible.

Total dependence on God also involves constant prayer, staying connected to Him as our guide and helper. Prayer is more than just asking God for things; it's a way of staying close to Him, sharing our hearts, and seeking His will in all we do. Philippians 4:6-7 encourages us, "Be careful for nothing; but in every thing by prayer and supplication with thanksgiving let your requests be made known unto God. And the peace of God, which passeth all understanding, shall keep your hearts and minds through Christ Jesus." When we depend on God, we bring every concern, every need, and every decision to Him in prayer, trusting that He hears us and will answer according to His perfect plan. This dependence allows us to experience God's peace, knowing that we have placed everything in His hands. Prayer becomes our lifeline, the way we stay grounded in His presence and aware of His guidance. It helps us to remember that we are not alone, that God is with us every step of the way, and that He is actively working in our lives, even when we cannot see it. Through prayer, we build a relationship with God that strengthens our faith and keeps us connected to His power and wisdom.

On this journey, total dependence on God also means relying on His wisdom, trusting that He knows what is best for us and for our mission. There will be times when we don't understand why things happen the way they do or why certain doors close, but depending on God means trusting His wisdom above our own. Isaiah 55:8-9 reminds us, "For my thoughts are not your thoughts, neither are your ways my ways, saith the Lord. For as the heavens are higher than the earth, so are my ways higher than your ways, and my thoughts than your thoughts." This verse encourages us to accept that God's understanding is far greater than ours and that His ways are beyond our comprehension. By depending on His wisdom, we can surrender our need to have all the answers and find peace in knowing that He is leading us according to His perfect plan. This trust allows us to let go of worry and fear, believing that God's wisdom will guide us through every decision and every challenge, even when we don't understand the "why" or "how."

Depending on God also requires us to surrender our plans and be willing to follow His lead, even if it means going in a direction we didn't expect. Sometimes, God's vision for us may take us down paths that seem difficult, uncomfortable, or even impossible. But total dependence means we are willing to follow Him, no matter where He leads. Luke 9:23 teaches, "And he said to them all, If any man will come after me, let him deny himself, and take up his cross daily, and follow me." This verse shows us that following Jesus requires self-denial, a willingness to let go of our own plans, and a heart that is fully surrendered to God's will. When we depend on God, we give Him control, trusting that He knows the best path for us and that He will lead us to where we need to be. This surrender is not always easy, but it brings us closer to God and allows us to experience His faithfulness in profound ways.

Total dependence on God also teaches us humility, helping us to recognize that all we have and all we accomplish comes from Him. It's easy to feel pride when things go well, to believe that our own efforts have brought success. But depending on God reminds us that everything we do is because of His grace and His provision. John 15:5 says, "I am the vine, ye are the branches: He that abideth in me, and I in him, the same bringeth forth much fruit: for without me ye can do nothing." This verse humbles us, showing that we are like branches that can only bear fruit if we remain connected to Jesus. When we depend on God, we realize that He is the source of our strength, our wisdom, and our ability to carry out His mission. This humility keeps us grounded, grateful, and aware of our need for Him in every aspect of our lives.

Ultimately, total dependence on God on this trail from vision to mission is about building a life that is rooted in trust, faith, and surrender. It's about recognizing that we are not meant to walk this journey alone, that God is our refuge, our strength, and our guide. This dependence brings us closer to Him, deepens our relationship with Him, and allows us to experience His love in deeper ways. Each step of dependence is a reminder that God is with us, that He is for us, and that He will provide everything we need to fulfill the mission He has placed in our hearts. This journey may be challenging, but with God's strength, we can accomplish all things, knowing that His power is made perfect in our weakness.

As we continue on this trail, may we learn to trust God completely, to depend on His strength for every step, and to walk in the assurance that He is our refuge and our guide. This is our calling, our purpose, and our joy—to live in total dependence on God, to rely on His strength, and to fulfill the mission He has given us with a heart of faith and surrender. This journey from vision to mission is a path that transforms us, strengthens our faith, and allows us to experience the fullness of God's love, grace, and power in every moment.

Chapter 25 - Treasuring the Call

The journey on the "Trail From Vision to Mission" reminds us to treasure the call that God has placed on our lives, seeing it as a precious and holy purpose that we are privileged to pursue. God's call is not something we take lightly or view as ordinary; it is a unique and precious mission designed by Him specifically for each of us, a path that leads us closer to His heart as we serve and love others. In Philippians 3:14, Paul writes, "I press toward the mark for the prize of the high calling of God in Christ Jesus." This verse shows us that God's calling is like a prize, a goal that is worth pursuing with all our heart and strength. Treasuring the call means we recognize that God has set us apart for something meaningful, something that brings glory to Him and hope to others. We value this call not because of our own greatness, but because God has entrusted us with it, inviting us to join Him in His work. Each step we take on this mission, each act of kindness, each word of encouragement, and each moment spent in service, becomes part of a divine purpose that reaches beyond ourselves. Treasuring the call means we don't see it as a burden or an obligation but as a gift, something to be embraced with gratitude, dedication, and a humble heart.

When we treasure God's call, we are willing to make sacrifices, to let go of things that may distract us, and to focus on the mission He has given us. This commitment might mean saying "no" to certain comforts or conveniences, but we do so joyfully, knowing that the purpose God has placed in our hearts is worth more than anything this world can offer. Matthew 6:21 reminds us, "For where your treasure is, there will your heart be also." When we value God's call as our treasure, our hearts are fully invested in His work, motivated by love and faith rather than duty. We find joy in serving, knowing that each moment spent on this mission is a moment spent with God, drawing us closer to Him and allowing us to experience His presence in new ways. Our priorities begin to shift as we align our hearts with His purpose, choosing to live for something eternal rather than temporary. Treasuring the call is about seeing our lives as part of a greater story, a story that God is writing, and being grateful that He has chosen us to play a part in it.

To treasure God's call means to carry it with a sense of reverence, understanding that this mission is sacred and significant. We approach each day with a heart ready to serve, knowing that our actions, words, and attitudes have the power to impact others and bring them closer to God. 1 Corinthians 15:58 encourages us, "Therefore, my beloved brethren, be ye stedfast, unmoveable, always abounding in the work of the Lord, forasmuch as ye know that your labour is not in vain in the Lord." This verse reassures us that our efforts are not wasted; every act of faithfulness and every step of obedience is valuable in God's sight. Treasuring the call means we are steadfast, unshaken by challenges, and committed to doing our best for the Lord. We don't let difficulties or discouragement keep us from the work He has given us because we know that it matters to Him. Our mission becomes a way to honor God, to show Him our love and devotion, and to reflect His goodness to those around us.

When we treasure God's call, we are also careful to protect it, guarding our hearts against anything that might lead us away from His purpose. This doesn't mean we live in fear, but rather, we live with a sense of awareness, choosing to focus on what strengthens our faith and deepens our commitment. Proverbs 4:23 advises us, "Keep thy heart with all diligence; for out of it are the issues of life." Treasuring the call means keeping our hearts centered on God, nurturing our relationship with Him through prayer, worship, and studying His Word, so that we stay connected to the vision He has given us. We avoid distractions, seek His guidance in all things, and stay rooted in His promises. By doing this, we create a strong foundation that helps us stay faithful to the mission, even when the path is difficult or the journey feels long. Treasuring the call means making God's purpose the most important thing in our lives, a priority that shapes our choices, our relationships, and our actions.

As we cherish the mission God has given us, we also find courage to press on, even when the road is hard. There will be moments when the mission feels challenging, when we face opposition, or when we feel weary. But when we truly value God's call, we find the strength to keep going, trusting that He will provide what we need. Isaiah 40:31 promises, "But they that wait upon the Lord shall renew their strength; they shall mount up with wings as eagles; they shall run, and not be weary; and they shall walk, and not faint." This verse reminds us that God renews our strength when we rely on Him, giving us the endurance to carry on. Treasuring the call means we don't give up, even in difficult times, because we know that God is with us, supporting us, and guiding us every step of the way. Our love for the mission He has given us becomes a source of courage, allowing us to face challenges with a spirit of hope and resilience.

Treasuring the call also fills us with joy, a joy that comes from knowing we are fulfilling God's purpose for our lives. This joy is not based on circumstances; it is a deep, abiding happiness that comes from being in alignment with God's will. Psalm 37:4 encourages us, "Delight thyself also in the Lord; and he shall give thee the desires of thine heart." When we treasure God's call, our delight is found in Him, and He fills our hearts with a joy that cannot be shaken. We find happiness in serving others, in making a difference, and in knowing that our lives are part of something greater than ourselves. This joy fuels our passion, making the work feel lighter, and reminding us that we are not alone in this mission. God's joy strengthens us, helping us to serve with a cheerful heart and a spirit of gratitude.

To value God's call means to live with a sense of purpose, knowing that every day offers new opportunities to make a difference. We become more aware of the people around us, more sensitive to their needs, and more willing to reach out in love. Colossians 3:23-24 encourages us, "And whatsoever ye do, do it heartily, as to the Lord, and not unto men; Knowing that of the Lord ye shall receive the reward of the inheritance: for ye serve the Lord Christ." This verse reminds us to serve with all our heart, knowing that our true reward comes from God. Treasuring the call means we don't seek recognition or applause; our satisfaction comes from knowing we are serving God, fulfilling His purpose, and making a difference in the lives of others. Our mission becomes a way to express our love for Him, and each act of kindness, no matter how small, becomes a meaningful part of His plan.

Ultimately, treasuring the call on this trail from vision to mission is about living each day with a heart of gratitude and dedication. We recognize that God has chosen us, that He has given us a mission filled with purpose, and that we are blessed to be part of His work. This journey becomes a precious gift, a path that brings us closer to God and allows us to experience His love in new and powerful ways. We treasure the call because it reminds us of who we are in Christ, beloved and chosen, with a purpose that goes beyond ourselves. As we continue on this journey, may we hold tightly to the mission God has given us, may we value it with all our heart, and may we fulfill it with joy, faithfulness, and a spirit of gratitude. This is our calling, our purpose, and our joy—to treasure God's call, to live each day with a heart fully devoted to His mission, and to bring His love to a world that desperately needs it. The journey from vision to mission is a path filled with meaning, transformation, and a deep connection to God's heart. We treasure this call, knowing that it is a gift from Him, and we walk this path with confidence, hope, and a steadfast commitment to the mission He has entrusted to us.

Conclusion

As we come to the close of "The Trail from Vision to Mission," I hope you feel a renewed sense of purpose and clarity about the journey God has set before you. The words from Lamentations 3:51, "Mine eye affecteth mine heart," remind us that what we allow ourselves to see—through God's lens—can shape our hearts profoundly. When our eyes are open to His vision, our hearts are stirred to action, and our lives become a living response to His call. Each chapter in this book has been a step toward transforming that vision into mission, equipping you to live out your faith with intentionality and love.

Throughout these chapters, we have explored how to let God's compassion, strength, and wisdom guide our every step. We've seen how a life shaped by His vision is one that reflects humility, resilience, and steadfast trust in His promises. No matter what stage of life you're in, no matter the size of the mission field God has called you to—whether it's within your family, your community, or beyond—you are now equipped with insights and actions to live a purpose-driven Christian life. You've been encouraged to build a foundation on His truth, nurture a compassionate heart, take bold steps of faith, and persevere in love, all while depending on His strength.

Living out this mission isn't always easy. The challenges may feel overwhelming at times, and there will be moments when you may question your ability or the impact you're making. But remember, God does not call you to act in your own strength; He calls you to depend on His. He promises to go with you, to empower you, and to work through you in ways beyond what you can imagine. As you walk this trail, trust that God is using every small act of obedience, every word of kindness, and every step of faith to make a difference. The journey may be long, but it's filled with purpose and led by a faithful God who treasures every effort made in His name.

As you continue from here, may you embrace the mission God has placed on your heart with a sense of reverence, joy, and commitment. Let each day be an opportunity to draw closer to Him, to listen to His voice, and to let His love guide your actions. The vision He has given you is a gift, a glimpse into the work He is doing in the world, and an invitation to join Him in that work. Treasure this call, for it is both a privilege and a responsibility.

May your eyes remain open to the needs around you, may your heart stay tender and responsive to His Spirit, and may your life be a beacon of His love and hope. Let your vision continue to move you to action, turning each step into a faithful journey toward fulfilling His purpose. As you walk from vision to mission, know that you are not alone—God goes before you, walks beside you, and strengthens you every step of the way. May your life reflect His light, inspiring others to find their own path from vision to mission, all for His glory.

Don't miss out!

Visit the website below and you can sign up to receive emails whenever Joshua Rhoades publishes a new book. There's no charge and no obligation.

https://books2read.com/r/B-A-AJLBB-WHTFF

BOOKS 2 READ

Connecting independent readers to independent writers.

Did you love *The Trail From Vision To Mission*? Then you should read *A Christmas Journey of Faith*[1] by Joshua Rhoades!

In "A Christmas Journey of Faith", join four friends—Jake, Emma, Max, and Maya—on a thrilling time-travel adventure. When they discover a mysterious time machine hidden in an old shed, they embark on an incredible journey that takes them over 2,000 years into the past to witness the most important event in history: the birth of Jesus Christ. But this journey isn't just about seeing the past—it's about learning timeless lessons of faith, trust, and courage.

As they travel back to the time of Mary and Joseph, the friends witness the Christmas story unfold. From the angel Gabriel's visit to Mary to the long journey to Bethlehem and the miraculous birth of Jesus in a humble stable, they find themselves in the heart of the greatest miracle. They stand in awe as the shepherds receive the good news from the angels, follow the star with the wise men, and learn how Mary and Joseph trusted God's plan, even when it was difficult.

---

1. https://books2read.com/u/bWA9Qz

2. https://books2read.com/u/bWA9Qz

Each step of their journey shows how faith in God can guide us through life's challenges. The friends learn that Christmas isn't about presents or decorations, but about the gift of Jesus, who came to bring peace, love, and hope to the world. As they experience these incredible events, they realize that God's love and salvation are for everyone—rich or poor, young or old.

"A Christmas Journey of Faith" is a heartwarming story that reminds readers of all ages to trust God's plan and embrace the true meaning of Christmas. Through the eyes of Jake, Emma, Max, and Maya, readers will be inspired to live out the message of salvation and faith that Jesus brought to the world.